To Rosalie

Enjoy the cooking!

Isabelle

To Rosalie

Enjoy the cooking!

[illegible]

perbaccoisabella!

Paesano's
RISTORANTE

perbaccoisabella!

italian country cooking from your good friends at paesano's

CHEF ISABELLA NICOLETTI

HURON RIVER PRESS

All inquiries should be addressed to:

Huron River Press
201 South Main Street, Suite 900
Ann Arbor, Michigan 48104
www.huronriverpress.com

Food photography: Mark Thomas, Grand Rapids, Michigan
Photography assistant: Bob Hazen
Food stylist: Loretta Gorman
Location photography: Steve Kuzma, Steven Klein, Shira Klein, Michael Roddy,
Piero Rasia, Roberta Cozza, Mike Savitski, Suzan Alexander
Family photographs courtesy of the Nicoletti family
Photograph on page 145 courtesy of Badia a Coltibuono
Book design: Savitski Design, Ann Arbor, Michigan

Printed and bound in China

10 9 8 7 6 5 4 3 2 1

Library of Congress Cataloging-in-Publication Data

Nicoletti, Isabella, 1969-
Perbacco Isabella! : Italian country cooking from your good friends at
Paesano's / by Isabella Nicoletti. -- 1st ed.
p. cm.
Includes bibliographical references and index.
ISBN 1-932399-13-5 (alk. paper)
1. Cookery, Italian. I. Title.
TX723.N533 2006
641.5'945--dc22
2006019667

We would like to thank and dedicate this project to all our loyal customers and our good friends (Paesanos), who have supported us and watched us evolve over the years. To all of our employees past and present, who have helped share and create our dream. To Dan Sutter, who has been our rock in the kitchen since the day we opened and has done everything we've ever asked of him, quietly, completely and successfully. To Chaad Thomas, our Wine Director, who has made Italian wine a part of all our lives. To Darla, Cindie, and Chris who keep our operations in check every day. To Salvatore Bisaccia, our Italian spark plug that keeps us all speaking Italian correctly. To Isabella's husband, Kevin, a fellow restaurant-lifer, who has stood by her side and supported her needs. Finally, to our family, Meagan, Maura, and Mia, the Roddy girls, who virtually grew up at the restaurant and are now all out of college and on with their lives. And a special dedication, to "Ya-Ya", Bridget's mother, Mary Sperrazza, whose Sicilian spirit still lives on here at Paesano's.

Thanks to all of you!

primavera

SPRING

estate

SUMMER

autunno

AUTUMN

inverno

WINTER

When we first envisioned Paesano's, terms like "mission statement" weren't so popular, but we had a dream, so back in 1984, we followed our "heart's desire" and opened a restaurant. It was to be an Italian restaurant that served heart healthy Italian foods using locally grown products. The foods and theme would be rustic, homey, Italian grandmother comfort fare that would change with the best offerings available seasonally. It would be family friendly, wine friendly and price friendly. We would get the community involved through Italian language classes, cooking and wine education, weekly wine tastings, and Italian wine maker dinners. We even dreamed of annual customer appreciation trips to Italy, exploring authentic foods and wines, region by region. But besides God, who would be our co-pilot, in fulfilling this mission, our heart's desire?

Thankfully, we have had many wonderful people work with us throughout the years and each one has helped us on this journey, but we still sought out that guide, that driver, that unique, special someone who shared our vision. In my discussion with a friend, the son of an Italian master chef, we were led to a recently immigrated Italian chef who told me he planned to leave the area, so he couldn't help me. But grabbing his jutted jaw, exhorted "I heard about this girl!" That simple statement led us to a corporate executive Italian chef who explained that the style of food we wished to serve was not his forte, but that we should check out "this girl!" Our curiosity was piqued; we had to find "this girl." Finally, a name, a contact, Isabella Nicoletti!

After meeting Isabella, we discovered that she was in search of a restaurant where she could fulfill her longing to do her authentic, unique, rustic foods inspired by her life in Italy. We, a restaurant in search of a chef to do just that, shared with her our mission and offered her a stage on which to create her foods. Isabella accepted the offer and we surrendered the kitchen. "This girl" has become "our girl." This dream has become our dream. During the past eight years, each and every part of our original mission has become reality, and we owe it all to "this girl!" Bringing out this cookbook to celebrate Isabella's favorite seasonal dishes is yet another dream realized, and we hope that you will enjoy the book, the food, but most of all, "this girl", Isabella!

Molto Grazie e Buon Appetito

Bridget Roddy Michael Roddy

Bridget and Michael Roddy

Ogni tanto mi soffermo a pensare a quanto sono riuscita a realizzare nel corso della mia carriera professionale. Sogni e fantasie hanno sempre fatto parte della mia vita e considerando che sono un po' testarda per la maggior parte sono riuscita a compiere quanto ho desiderato. Di sicuro, mai avrei pensato che un giorno avrei avuto il MIO LIBRO DI CUCINA! Per questo senz'altro devo ringraziare le persone che mi stanno attorno condividendo i miei stessi sogni e che hanno fiducia e ammirazione nel mio lavoro.

Mike e Bridget prima di tutti, con i quali ho un speciale rapporto di lavoro e amicizia e grazie ai quali ho avuto la possibilitá, in questi anni, di esprimere con il cibo la mia personalitá.

Con questo libro posso dire che tutte le mie fatiche, frustrazioni e soprattutto il duro lavoro di vent'anni sono state appagate, e senza dubbio ho la conferma che sogni e fantasie possono diventare realtá.

The Wine of Italy's Veneto Region

One of my most memorable wine experiences occurred in a bar in Venice. Although I'd done my obligatory Venetian tour, my girlfriend had not, and so I found myself sweltering one July afternoon somewhere deep in the city's ancient maze of canals and cobblestone. Of course, we were lost. We'd been masquerading as knowledgeable insiders for hours, pretending to have a reason for our wandering, but finally we had faded, and so ducked into a small bar for respite.

While my companion headed for the restroom, I headed to the bar, imagining nothing more refreshing than a simple, cold glass of local white. In Italian, I asked the bartender for a glass of white wine, "Un bicchiere di vino bianco, per favore!" I'd grown up with Italian, and with three Italian trips under my belt, I was pretty confident that my pronunciation and manner didn't give me away immediately as an outsider. I could've been a remnant from Italy's desultory and imprudent colonization efforts in Ethiopia, right?

No matter, because as soon as I saw the barkeeper grab a juice glass and head to the tap, my fanciful imaginings ground to a halt. As I watched him pour what looked like a rather light beer into the glass, I replayed my request, wondering what would have made him think that I wanted a beer. Set in front of me, it became immediately clear that this bubbling liquid was not beer, but in fact, a wine indeed! I hadn't been thinking bubbles, but I was damn hot and thirsty, and it looked good.

And what a marvelous surprise the lightly fruity and refreshing beverage was! I downed it pretty quickly, and asked the bartender what it was, and for another glass. I was enjoying my second glass of prosecco by the time my girlfriend returned from the restroom.

Maybe that experience was profoundly American. There was a time, back in the days of Carlo Rossi, Blue Nun, Mateus, and Ripple, when white Italian wine from the Veneto was the most popular wine in the nation. That wine was Bolla Soave, and from its humble beginnings near the town of Soave, not far from Verona, it grew into a success model that set the benchmark for the region as a whole. Unfortunately, while that model was viable for short term success, it soon put the region out-of-sync with more dominant trends in the global industry. In short, the leading wine producing regions were focusing on quality, while Veneto focused on quantity.

Today, however, the picture is very different, and the Veneto region is among Italy's most exciting wine zones, and therefore also a world leader. Once abused or neglected grape varieties, like the garganega of Soave fame, are now at the center of renewed attention and respect. Other native varieties like corvina, raboso, prosecco, molinara, oseletta and verduzzo deepen the pool of fine, regional wines.

The Veneto is blessed with more than just a wealth of grape varieties. A select few wine regions in the world are distinguished by their winemaking techniques: Sauternes in France with botrytis, and the icewines of

Germany's Rhine valley come readily to mind. In the Veneto, winemakers use the apassimento, or drying of grapes after harvest, to craft the powerful, unique, wine of Amarone, which is certainly the region's most prestigious wine. The drying of the grapes, usually done on bamboo mats in ventilated second-story rooms, concentrates the juice, imparting thicker texture, as well as raisin, chocolate, leather, and black pepper notes to a wine light-years away from its made-from-fresh-juice brother, Valpolicella.

Led by the Masi winery, this process is being applied in new ways, such as in the drying of the white wine grape verduzzo for the production of their Masianco wine. But even for wineries that are not pioneering winemaking techniques, a newly-found dedication to meticulous winemaking practices such as green harvesting to reduce yields, organic farming, and minimal filtering and handling means that general quality is very, very good indeed.

While many of the recipes in this book have specific pairing recommendations, keep in mind that there are many alternative choices, and that vintages come and go in any case. Besides being incumbent upon every wine lover to try as many wines as possible, the explorer in Italy generally, and the Veneto particularly, will be amply rewarded with unforgettable, inimitable wines of profound character!

Chaad Thomas
Wine Director

You Must Read This and You Must Read This Now!

Just a few words I would like to say to explain how to handle this book. You won't see any recipe (well, maybe a couple!) that you would recognize in other Italian cookbooks. The appetizers, salads, pastas and entrees are definitely, for the most part, my own creations, to the exception of some typical dishes. Few of these recipes require more than one step and I have no doubt that anyone can prepare them; just realize that you must read carefully top to bottom, the whole "project" before getting your hands dirty! Many of my recipes call for steps and/or preparations that could be done 2–3 days before you actually want to use them. I don't want to drive people crazy either, trying to find the exact special ingredients. Sometimes you need to use your own imagination and I'm sure you can come up with a great solution!

Reading through and making some recipes, you'll see that some leftovers will be part of "the program," not to worry! It can all be frozen (from sauces, to raw gnocchi or dumplings) and used for the same recipe in the future or for whatever treat you can come up with. Never try or share a new recipe to "strangers" or at special events. You'll never know how it can turn out. You must cook it for yourself and family first, before you offer it to others, unless of course, you are very talented (or very brave) and you know what you are doing.

Now, going through the list of things that might be a little confusing, let's start with:

Blanch Bring salted water to a boil, drop in vegetables and stir quickly. Then, shock them in an ice bath to preserve color and crunchiness.

Bread Challah, white, whole wheat, for the most part you can substitute as you wish, but I cannot say that the end result of the recipe will be as good as the original!

Bread flour 90% of the time it will be okay to substitute all-purpose flour.

Butter It's never salted! Sweet or unsalted works just fine.

Butterfly Split open without cutting all the way through.

Caul fat A thin fatty membrane that lines the abdominal cavity, usually from sheep or pigs; pork caul is considered the best. It looks like a lacy net and is used to wrap and contain pates and such to hold their shape during cooking. The membrane melts during the cooking adding fat to baste the food. You may have to soak the membrane in warm salted water to loosen the layers before using. You can get it from your butcher.

De-bearded Take the beard off! The fuzzy stuff, you know? Always make sure to rinse off mussels after that.

De-stemmed Take it off the stem!

Frying temperature When you get the oil hot, *do not* put your finger in it! Instead, you could drop a piece of bread and if it sizzles, the temperature is right!

Ice bath A pan filled halfway with water, with 2–3 cups of added ice to it.

Immersion blender Nothing to do with the hand mixer! This is a hand emulsion tool. A blender or food processor are good alternatives.

Julienne Thinly sliced.

NV Non vintage...for all you who think you know it all!

Oven It is always preheated! So, if you come across a recipe that doesn't say it, well, sorry. I guess we thought you knew!

Slotted spoon A big, wide, preferably perforated spoon able to catch 3–4 wide dumplings at a time.

Timbale/Ramekins Little dishes to make custards in. To unmold them dip in hot, hot water for a few seconds, then turn upside down on the plate. If it doesn't come out, put the tip of a knife between the mold and "custard" to create an air pocket. That should do it!

Waterbath It means whatever you are cooking you must put it in a bigger container so that you can pour water around it and halfway up the sides. Then just cook it!

Hopefully, I gave you enough tips for you to be able to cook my recipes without scratching your head too much. Probably, I'm missing something, but...what the heck! Use your imagination!

Spring may be my favorite season; everything comes back to life. The first flowers are coming out of the ground, le "primole", a primrose and o "bucaneve," a little flower that pokes up through the snow.

My papá, mamma, my sorella Graziella and I would go picking "bruscandoli," a wild asparagus or "tarassaco," dandelion, very tender and very tasty. My mamma would sauté and freeze them in small batches to enjoy their special taste in the future when they are overgrown, so bitter.

Of course, our house would have a lot of rabbit and lamb, light ricotta gnocchi, asparagus and ramps — all the firsts of the season. Tart lemon desserts would brighten our table and our mouths. The cold weather was behind us, Easter was around the corner and finally I got to enjoy an afternoon sitting on the house steps looking at the flowers and searching for the first lizards.

primavera

SPRING

For the Liver

1 lb calf's liver, from local butcher, cleaned
4 tbsp butter
pinch of salt and pepper
1 cup Marsala wine
Polenta Bianca (see page 20)
Custard (see below)

For the Custard

1 large onion, sliced
1 cup heavy cream
3 egg yolks
¾ tsp salt
pinch of black pepper
5 4 oz metal baking cups or ramekins

ANTIPASTO — SERVES 5

Fegato e cipolle

CALF'S LIVER AND ONION CUSTARD

Calf's liver and onions is a dish that is eaten all over Northern Italy. My mamma would prepare this all the time and it is truly one of my favorite memories of home. Here again, I've added my "twist" on the classic dish by using the sautéed onions for a custard. I've left the liver preparation in the the traditional cooking style. This way I have a little of home and a little of the creative me.

The Polenta Bianca should be made the day before. The custard could be made the day before — just reheat in the oven for about 20-30 minutes.

FOR THE LIVER

1 Cut the liver into small slices. Preheat a pan, add 2 tbsp butter and let heat until it starts sizzling. Add the liver, let cook for 2-3 minutes stirring occasionally. Season with a pinch of salt and pepper.

2 When the liver appears cooked from all sides add the Marsala wine and let it partially evaporate. Keeping at a high heat, add about 2 tbsp of chilled butter. This will help thicken the sauce. Make sure to keep shaking the pan until all the butter is incorporated.

FOR THE CUSTARD

3 Using a steamer, cook the onions until they are well done, translucent and soft. Then let them cool.

4 In a bowl, mix the cream with the egg yolks and the seasoning.

5 Using a food processor purée the onions. Pour ¾ cup of it into the cream mixture and stir well.

6 Butter or spray the baking cups or ceramic ramekins. Divide the mixture between them. Put them into a water bath (see page 15). Bake in a preheated oven at 350°F for about 45 minutes. The top will become golden and when shaken the filling will appear firm; which means it is ready. Take out of the oven and set aside.

FOR THE PRESENTATION

7 Turn the baking cups upside down on each plate (see pg 15). Divide the liver between the plates. Finish with the sauce and serve with fried polenta cubes (see page 20).

WINE PAIRING '01 FELSINA CHIANTI CLASSICO RISERVA "RANCIO"

3 cups water
1 tsp salt
2 tbsp olive oil
1 cups grits
semolina flour, for dredging
oil for frying

CONTORNO — SERVES 4-6

Polenta Bianca

WHITE POLENTA CUBES

It is almost a workout "fare la polenta" [making the polenta]. Stirring yes, but you can take a break once in a while, as long as there is not film forming on top.

1 Bring the water and seasonings to a boil, and then slightly lower the heat while you whisk in the grits. Otherwise, the grits will splatter. Keep stirring until the grits get thicker. Lower the heat further and let cook for 20-25 minutes stirring once in a while with a wooden spoon.

2 Spray or brush a small pan (about 9 x 9 inches). Pour in the polenta and cover with plastic wrap to avoid any crust on top. Let cool completely. Turn the pan upside down to remove polenta and cut into ¾-inch cubes. When you are ready, dredge the cubes in semolina flour and fry in oil until golden in color on all sides.

Io e mia sorella Graziella, 1970

4	tbsp butter
6	garlic cloves, cut into smaller pieces
2½	cups heavy cream
10	oz Gorgonzola cheese
15	oz sourdough or challah bread
¼	tsp salt
⅛	tsp pepper
4	eggs

ANTIPASTO — SERVES 10-12

Budino di Pane al Gorgonzola

GORGONZOLA BREAD PUDDING

I personally like the bread pudding more the day after it has been made because I love the "crusty" look you get from baking it twice in the oven. Simply slice it and then rebake it!

By the way, Budino means pudding!

1 Into a small pan melt the butter and add the garlic. Let cook for a couple of minutes, then add the heavy cream and bring to a boil.

2 Remove from the stove and using a whisk, add the Gorgonzola. Stir until the cheese melts. Let sit for a few minutes, while you prepare the bread.

3 After taking the crust off, dice the bread into cubes, about ¾ inches and put them into a bowl.

4 Add the seasonings and eggs into the cream mixture, whisking very well to mix all the ingredients. Pour it over the bread and let it soak for 15–20 minutes.

5 Preheat the oven to 350°F.

6 Butter a small bread loaf pan, 8 x 4 inches. Put the bread mixture into the pan after allowing it to soak.

7 Place the bread pan into a water bath (see page 15). Bake uncovered for about 45 minutes to 1 hour or until the top is golden and you can see that the cream mixture has been absorbed. Remove from the oven and let cool while in the water pan.

8 You can cut it and eat it right away or just refrigerate the pudding and use it even after a couple days. Just make sure to slice it and reheat it in the oven at a higher temperature, 450°F to heat through.

WINE PAIRING '03 AVIGNONESI ROSSO

For the Rabbit

1 rabbit, cut into pieces
2 tbsp kosher salt
⅛ tsp ground black pepper
2 juniper berries, crushed
2 bay leaves, crushed
1 tsp fresh garlic, chopped
duck fat, to cover rabbit

For the Quenelles

7 oz ramps or leeks, cleaned and chopped in small dice
2 tbsp butter
½ oz dry morels, soaked in hot water
rabbit meat, cooked
Béchamel Sauce (see recipe below)
10 fresh sage leaves
2 tbsp butter. melted

For the Béchamel Sauce

1 cup milk
2 oz roux (2 tbsp butter and 2 tbsp flour combined to make a paste)
pinch of salt and pepper

ANTIPASTO — SERVES 6

Gnocchi di Confit di Coniglio

RABBIT CONFIT QUENELLES

Rabbit, of course, is very symbolic of spring. I think of it as one might think of duck or goose in the fall. This dish has an unusual preparation that requires you to cook the rabbit in duck fat. Many butchers will have it readily available, but you may want to call ahead in case you need to pre-order it. You will need to melt down the fat in a pot. It can be stored in the refrigerator for a long time. When you need it, you will have to melt it again before pouring on the item you are preparing.

FOR THE RABBIT

1 Place the rabbit pieces into a pan. Combine the rest of the dry ingredients and sprinkle all over the meat. Cover with plastic wrap and weight it by placing a plate with some cans on top. Let it sit in the refrigerator for at least 36 hours.

2 Clean off the rabbit, by wiping it. Place it into a clean baking pan. Cover with the melted duck fat and roast in a preheated oven until well done, about an hour at 350°F. Let cool off, remove the fat and pull the meat off the bones.

FOR THE QUENELLES

3 Sauté the ramps in 1 tbsp of butter until well done, then set aside.

4 Drain the morels, chop them very fine and sauté them in 1 tbsp of butter for 3-4 minutes. Set aside until cool.

5 Using a food processor chop the ramps, morels and rabbit meat. Add the Béchamel Sauce and adjust the seasoning if necessary. Using 2 dinner spoons scoop and shape the quenelles into an oval shape.

FOR THE BÉCHAMEL SAUCE

6 To boiling milk, add roux stirring with a whisk. Turn heat to simmer for about 15 minutes until thickened. Add salt and pepper and remove from heat.

FOR THE PRESENTATION

7 Whenever ready to serve the quenelles, you should reheat them in the oven and drizzle with hot melted butter and fresh sage.

WINE PAIRING '01 SELLA & MOSCA CANNONAU DI SARDEGNA RISERVA

Carnevale

One harbinger of spring at Paesano's is Carnevale, a dazzling Mardi Gras celebration held annually on "Fat Tuesday". This Italian holiday dates back to the 11 th century and has always been a time of excitement and merriment for all and a last "fling" before the rigors of Lent. It was time to feast on the last of winter's supply of meat and an opportunity for people to put on costumes and forget who they are [and behave any way they wanted].

At Paesano's, we close the dining room to accommodate the overflow crowd and Isabella creates an unbelievable menu as Chaad pairs the perfect wines. Strolling minstrels, festive décor, magical entertainment, and the fellowship of good friends donned in costumes make it a memorable evening.

For the Pizza

1 ball of pizza dough (see page 166)
3 oz Garlic Sauce (see recipe below)
½ cup ramps (wild leeks)
½ cup morel mushrooms
½ cup asparagus, thinly sliced
3 oz mozzarella, shredded
¼ oz fresh tarragon leaves

For the Garlic Sauce

2 heads of garlic, peeled
1 cup heavy cream
½ cup milk
1 tsp salt
⅛ tsp white pepper

ANTIPASTO — YIELD 1 PIZZA

Pizza Primaverile

SPRING PIZZA WITH SPRING VEGETABLES AND FRESH MOREL MUSHROOMS

As you can imagine, Italy is well known for its pizza pies! All over Italy you will find Pizzerie, restaurants that serve pizzas with your choice of toppings. I've included a spring and winter version for the cookbook. You can use them as a starting point for your own creations and of course, they can be served year round.

Good idea to make the Garlic Sauce the day before.

FOR THE PIZZA

1 Preheat oven to 500°F.

2 Roll pizza on floured surface about 10 inches in diameter and place on baking sheet. Bake in oven for 4–5 minutes.

3 Take out and spread the garlic sauce on it. Top with ramps, morels, and asparagus. Sprinkle cheese on top. Bake for 10–12 minutes. Rotate the pizza once in a while to get a more uniform color on the crust.

4 When the pizza is ready, pull it from the oven, and sprinkle with tarragon. Cut into slices and serve.

FOR THE GARLIC SAUCE

5 Steam the garlic in a vegetable steamer over water until soft. Meanwhile, bring the cream to a boil with the milk and let simmer for 5–7 minutes. Add the garlic and purée to a smooth consistency. Season with salt and pepper.

WINE PAIRING '02 CAPUTO GRECO DI TUFO

For the Shells

1 single layer frozen tart shell or
8 4-inch frozen pie shells

For the Filling

12 oz asparagus (a little less than a bunch), ends trimmed and cleaned
2 tbsp butter
1 tsp fresh garlic, minced
1¼ cup white wine
3 eggs
1 cup heavy cream

ANTIPASTO — SERVES 8

Torta di Asparagi

COUNTRY ASPARAGUS TART

In Bassano, near Vicenza, every spring a big fair takes place to celebrate the famous white asparagus! It is slightly more delicate than the green and seen far less frequently. When asparagus starts appearing in the marketplace you know that spring is here!

FOR THE SHELLS

1 Bake the tart shell(s) at 350°F for 10–15 minutes or until it starts to color. Make sure to weigh down the pastry by laying a sheet of foil with beans on it so the crust won't rise.

FOR THE FILLING

2 Small dice the asparagus and sauté them in a pan with the melted butter and the garlic. Let cook for a couple of minutes. Add the wine and simmer until the asparagus is soft.

3 In a separate bowl crack the eggs and mix them with the cream. Put the asparagus mixture into the pie shell and fill it with the custard.

4 Bake in 450°F preheated oven for 25 minutes. Let cool slightly before serving.

FOR THE PRESENTATION

5 Arrange radicchio leaf and a small bunch of parsley alongside a slice of the tart for garnish.

WINE PAIRING '04 ARGIOLAS VERMENTINO "COSTAMOLINO"

For the Salad

½ cup pine nuts
1 lb asparagus (1 bunch), preferably "pencil" size, ends removed
2 tbsp olive oil
salt and pepper for seasoning
5 cups spinach leaves
1 lemon (zest only)
½ cup Shallot Vinaigrette (see recipe below)
1 cup fresh ricotta or goat cheese

For the Shallot Vinaigrette

1½ lemons, zested and juiced
1 cup shallots, peeled and minced
2 tbsp Dijon mustard
½ cup olive oil
½ cup extra virgin olive oil

INSALATA — SERVES 4

Insalata di Spinaci e Pinoli

RICOTTA, PINENUTS AND SPINACH SALAD

FOR THE SALAD

1 Preheat the oven to 350°F. Lay pine nuts on a baking sheet and toast them in the oven for about 20 minutes or until they are slightly colored.

2 Trim asparagus to 2-inch pieces. If they are thick, cut them in half lengthwise.

3 Heat the oil in a large skillet. Drop the asparagus spears and let them cook until they get nicely roasted, with a charred look all around. Season with salt and pepper and set aside.

4 Put the spinach in a bowl; add pine nuts, zest and vinaigrette. Toss well.

FOR THE SHALLOT VINAIGRETTE

5 Make sure you have ¾ cup of juice and ¼ cup of zest. Combine the lemon products and shallots in a small bowl and add the mustard and vinegar. Slowly drizzle in both oils while stirring with a whisk. Store in a covered container in the refrigerator.

FOR THE PRESENTATION

6 Divide onto 4 plates. Put ricotta on top of each salad, using your fingers to break it apart. Place the asparagus on top.

WINE PAIRING '02 BOTROMAGNO "GRAVINA"

For the Salad

1 cup asparagus, ends removed
1 cup frozen sweet peas, defrosted
5 cups mixed greens
½ cup ricotta salata, shaved
2 cups toasted croutons
¾ cup Honey Dressing, warm (see recipe below)

For the Honey Dressing

1 cup honey
½ cup rice wine vinegar
½ tsp salt
pinch of ground pepper
1¼ cups extra virgin olive oil

INSALATA — SERVES 4

Insalata Panzanella

SPRING PANZANELLA SALAD

Ricotta salata is an aged cheese usually made from sheep milk. Its younger version, ricotta, is often seen in desserts because of its creamy texture. The ripened version, ricotta salata, can be grated as in this recipe. If you cannot find it, use some Pecorino Romano instead. Quick, easy, buona!

FOR THE SALAD

1 Cut asparagus very thin on a bias.

2 Put greens in a bowl; add asparagus, defrosted peas, cheese and croutons.

FOR THE PRESENTATION

3 Mix together and divide salad onto 4 plates. Drizzle with the honey dressing.

FOR THE HONEY DRESSING

4 Mix all ingredients but the oil together. Slowly whisk in the oil.

5 Store in a covered container in the refrigerator. Warm up when ready to use.

WINE PAIRING '04 CA'MONTINI SAUVIGNON "L'ARISTOCRATICO"

For the Ricotta Gnocchi

1 lb ricotta
1 cup Parmigiano Reggiano cheese, grated
4 eggs
1 cup bread flour
½ tbsp salt
½ tsp white pepper

For the Sauce

4 tbsp butter
1 bunch fresh asparagus, ends removed, cut into slivers
1½ cups fresh morels, washed thoroughly
1½ cups clean sweetbreads
salt and pepper to taste
½ cup red wine
4 tbsp beef stock

PASTA — SERVES 5-6

Gnocchi di Ricotta con Funghi ed Animelle

RICOTTA GNOCCHI WITH MORELS AND SWEETBREADS

You will find the ricotta gnocchi to be a "lighter" gnocchi than the potato gnocchi we eat in the winter. They are very versatile; you can make them with any sauce you like as long as you keep it light and delicate.

If gnocchi are not keeping the shape, you might need to add a little more flour to the mixture.

FOR THE RICOTTA GNOCCHI

1 Mix all the ingredients together using a wooden spoon.

2 Bring a pot of water to a boil (and don't forget to add some salt to it!). Using an ice cream scoop, shape mixture into balls and drop them in the water. Don't have the water boiling too hard; otherwise the gnocchi will explode. Just turn the flame down and make sure they cook for at least 4-5 minutes. You could cook the gnocchi and then reheat them in fresh boiling water or keep the mixture refrigerated and use it when you are ready to eat. The recipe should yield about 30 gnocchi.

FOR THE SAUCE

3 Melt 2 tbsp of butter in a large pan until it starts to sizzle. Add the asparagus, morels and sweetbreads and let cook for a couple of minutes. Season with salt and pepper. Add the wine and beef stock and bring to a boil.

4 At this point, add the leftover butter (2 tbsp), cut into small pieces. While shaking the pan back and forth, make sure it gets well incorporated into the sauce.

FOR THE PRESENTATION

5 Pour sauce on bottom of plate and divide gnocchi evenly on top.

WINE PAIRING '03 CORTE ALLA FLORA ROSSO DI MONTEPULCIANO

For the Procedure

½ cup olive oil
12 large shrimp, peeled and deveined
1½ cups cooked lobster meat, cut into small pieces
¾ cup sweet frozen peas
¾ cup mozzarella, shredded
½ cup ricotta cheese
pinch of salt and pepper
6 pieces fresh pasta sheets, 6 x 6 inches
2 tbsp butter, melted
Lemon Cream Sauce (see recipe below)
½ bunch asparagus, cut on a bias

For the Lemon Cream Sauce

1 quart heavy cream
2 garlic cloves, minced
3 small lemons, juiced and strained, zest removed
¼ tsp salt and pepper

PASTA — SERVES 6

Fagotto con Gamberi ed Aragosta

HANDKERCHIEF SHRIMP PACKET

The preparation of this dish can be done in stages, first the filling and then the pasta, and then putting it together. You can do part or all of it the day before you need it.

FOR THE PROCEDURE

1 Heat oil in a pan and cook shrimp until done. Let cool and chop them into small pieces.

2 Combine the rest of the ingredients, except pasta and butter, in a bowl and mix well.

3 Meanwhile, bring a small pot of water to a boil with a little salt and cook the pasta sheets. It will be very fast, only 2–3 minutes. Have an ice bath ready so you can transfer the pasta in it to stop it from cooking longer. Lay out the sheets on the table, divide the mixture between all and fold the edges of the pasta around the filling. Turn them upside down and transfer to a parchment lined sheet pan.

4 Preheat oven to 450°F. Brush each packet with melted butter and put the pan in the oven and bake for about 25 minutes or until golden brown.

5 Heat oil in a pan and when hot, place asparagus and sauté for 2–3 minutes until slightly tender. Season with salt and pepper and set aside.

FOR THE LEMON CREAM SAUCE

6 Heat the cream and garlic together and reduce by ⅓. When the cream is ready add the lemon juice and zest. Then, add the salt and pepper and bring it to a boil. Pour into a container and store in refrigerator until ready to use.

FOR THE PRESENTATION

7 Reheat the Lemon Cream Sauce and ladle on serving plate. Place packet on top and garnish with sautéed slices of asparagus.

WINE PAIRING '04 MARIO SCHIOPETTO PINOT BIANCO

- 1 lamb shoulder, boneless
- 3 garlic cloves, peeled
- 1 tbsp fresh sage
- 1 tbsp fresh oregano
- 1 tbsp fresh thyme
- 1 cup olive oil
- 2 cups white wine
- vegetable or chicken stock
- salt and pepper, for seasoning
- 1 carrot
- 2 stalks of celery
- 1 small onion
- 1 small bunch of parsley
- 1½ lbs pappardelle or other dry pasta, cooked according to directions

PASTA — SERVES 7-8

Pappardelle con L'Agnello

PAPPARDELLE WITH ROASTED SPRING LAMB

If you want to make this sauce a little spicy, add some slivers of red cherry peppers to the vegetables before adding the meat.

1 Preheat oven to 350°F.

2 Finely chop garlic and fresh herbs. Rub them all around the meat. Put the meat in a baking pan with ½ cup of olive oil. Place in the oven and let roast for about 1 hour.

3 Remove pan from oven and add the wine and vegetable or chicken stock to cover halfway. Then cover the pan with aluminum foil and let roast in oven until well done.

4 Take the meat out of the juice, saving all of the juice. Let cool for a few minutes.

5 Small dice the carrot, celery, and onion and chop the parsley. Cook all in a pot with ½ cup of olive oil. Let cook 2-3 minutes. Meanwhile, small dice the meat and add it to the vegetables. Then, add the juice from roasting and let simmer together 5-10 minutes. Adjust seasoning with salt and pepper and store until ready to use.

FOR THE PRESENTATION

6 Prepare pasta according to directions, drain from water. Divide pasta into equal portions and top with roasted spring lamb sauce.

WINE PAIRING '01 ALTESINO "ROSSO DI ALTESINO"

For the Pasta

8–10 oz uncooked pasta or 16–20 oz cooked

For the Soft Shell Crabs

- Garlic Sauce (see page 25)
- ½ cup olive oil
- all-purpose flour, for dredging, if desired
- 12 soft shell crabs
- salt and pepper
- 4 tbsp butter
- 1 cup fresh morels, cleaned

PASTA — SERVES 4

Stracci di Pasta con Salsa all'Aglio e Granchio

PASTA "RAGS" WITH SWEET GARLIC SAUCE, CRABS & MOREL MUSHROOMS

FOR THE PASTA

1 Go to any specialty store or big market and in the fresh/frozen produce section you should find a selection of pastas. Buy the lasagna sheets and cut them into wide irregular strips. This is what makes the "rags". If, for any reason you cannot find fresh pasta, just buy the frozen or dry one, but keep in mind you won't be able to make them into "rags" until after they are cooked.

FOR THE SOFT SHELL CRABS

2 Bring a pot of water to boiling. In a smaller pot reheat the garlic sauce.

3 In a large pan warm up the oil. Lay soft shell crabs on one side and let cook for 2–3 minutes. You could flour them to get a crispier outside, but it is really not necessary. Flip over to the other side and cook for 2–3 minutes more. Sprinkle lightly with salt and pepper then set aside.

4 Using the same pan (wiping out if you used flour) add the butter and when it starts to sizzle add morels, cooking for 2–3 minutes. Turn off the heat.

5 Add a little salt to boiling water and cook pasta until al dente. Reserve some of the cooking water. Add pasta to the morels, toss it and if necessary, add some of the water to keep it from sticking to the pan.

FOR THE PRESENTATION

6 When ready to serve, put the Garlic Sauce on the bottom of the 4 pasta bowls and divide stracci between all. Top at the end with 3 soft shell crabs.

WINE PAIRING '04 CUSUMANO NERO D'AVOLA

For the Stuffing
2 tbsp olive oil
½ small onion, chopped very fine
1 lb fresh rhubarb, diced small
¾ cup raisins
¼ cup sugar
pinch of salt and pepper
½ cup breadcrumbs

For the Chicken Breasts
6 6–7 oz cleaned, boneless chicken breasts
½ cup of flour, for dredging
1 cup olive oil
4 tbsp butter
12 oz ramps or leeks
salt and pepper
Moscato Sauce (see recipe below)

For the Moscato Sauce
1 bottle moscato wine
1 cup homemade chicken stock or 1 tsp chicken base and 1 cup water
pinch of salt and pepper
1 oz roux (1 tbsp flour and 1 tbsp soft butter combined to make a paste)

CARNE — SERVES 6

Rollotini di Pollo Farciti al Rabarbaro con Salsa al Moscato

RHUBARB STUFFED CHICKEN ROLLS

Rhubarb is more often used in sauces in Italy than in desserts, as it is here in America. I have mixed it with raisins and sugar to sweeten it and added the savory onions to balance the flavor. The Moscato sauce is the perfect topping to complement the sweetened filling.

FOR THE STUFFING

1 Sauté the onions in a pan with the oil until translucent. Add the rhubarb and raisins. Let cook a couple of minutes. Add sugar, salt and pepper. Lower the heat and cook until the rhubarb is soft. Using the food processor purée the mixture. Put it in a container, add breadcrumbs, mix well and refrigerate until ready to use.

FOR THE CHICKEN BREASTS

2 Cut the breasts in half horizontally and pound them thin. Spread about ⅓ cup of the stuffing on each breast then roll them up. Heat oil in a large skillet, dredge each roll in flour and sear in the hot oil until they are golden brown. Place on a baking sheet and cook for about 25–30 minutes at 450°F.

3 In a separate pan, melt 2 tbsp of butter, add ramps and season with salt and pepper and cook for 4–5 minutes. Add the Moscato Sauce and bring it to a boil. Then add the rest of the butter, cut into small pieces and shake the pan back and forth to make sure it is all incorporated.

FOR THE MOSCATO SAUCE

4 Reduce the wine to ⅔ in a small pot. Add chicken stock and seasoning. Bring to a boil and using a whisk add roux and stir it until it all dissolves and thickens. Let boil for 2–3 minutes.

FOR THE PRESENTATION

5 Plate chicken rolls and pour sauce on top of chicken. Roasted potatoes and a side of roasted asparagus would complement the dish.

WINE PAIRING '04 FIRRIATO GRILLO "ALTAVILLA DELLA CORTE"

Pollame

Definitely, lots of fowl in the Veneto region. Mostly, we eat pheasant, hen, duck, and goose. We don't eat as much chicken as Americans do because all the other stuff has much more taste and flavor.

When I was a child we raised chickens, mostly for their eggs. When they were plump enough to eat I would help my mamma and papá kill them. My job was to pull out the guts and clean the intestines with vinegar. My mamma would prepare a wonderful stew. Today, the Italians have learned to prepare chickens in so many ways: broiled, baked, stewed, on a spit, breaded, sautéed, pounded and stuffed and pan roasted. My favorite way of eating chicken is still oven-roasted.

CARNE — SERVES 6

Galletto alla Griglia

GRILLED MARINATED POUSSIN

To me, there is nothing better than the flavor you get from grilling fowl on the grill. The skin gets so crispy and so tasty I can hardly wait until it's done to eat!

For the Marinade

- 6 10–12 oz squab or Cornish hen, split open taking backbone out
- 1 tbsp fresh sage, chopped
- 1 tbsp fresh rosemary, chopped
- 1 tbsp fresh parsley, chopped
- 1 tbsp fresh oregano, chopped
- 6 garlic cloves, minced
- ½ cup extra virgin olive oil

For the Procedure

- salt and pepper
- 4 tbsp butter
- 2 heads broccolini (12 oz), separate heads from stems and cut the stems on the bias
- 1½ cups sweetbreads
- ½ cup Balsamic Glaze (see page 176)
- Polenta Bianca cubes (see page 20)

FOR THE MARINADE

1 Combine the finely chopped herbs and garlic with the extra virgin olive oil and place in a bowl. Add the birds, tossing the herb mixture all around them. Cover with plastic wrap and refrigerate overnight.

FOR THE PROCEDURE

2 Get the grill hot and start cooking the meat alternating sides every 2-3 minutes. It will take about 20-25 minutes. Once you have cooked them halfway, season with salt and fresh ground pepper on both sides. While they are grilling, prepare the topping.

3 Melt the butter in a large pan until it starts to sizzle, add the broccolini, both heads and stems and sauté for 4-5 minutes. Add the sweetbreads and let cook for an additional 2-3 minutes. Season with salt and pepper.

FOR THE PRESENTATION

4 Display the squab or hen on each plate, divide polenta between all and finish with the vegetable and sweetbread topping. Then, drizzle with the Balsamic Glaze.

WINE PAIRING '99 SCILIO ETNA ROSSO "ORPHEUS"

1 cup long grain rice
2 lbs asparagus (2 bunches), ends removed
2 oranges
2 tbsp extra virgin olive oil
1 tsp salt
¼ tsp ground pepper
2 lbs large sea scallops
6 sheets parchment paper, about 24 x 16 inches

PESCE — SERVES 6

Capesante al Cartoccio

SCALLOP IN PARCHMENT WITH ORANGE ZEST

Very simple to make, just be sure to fold the parchment paper well. Definitely a nice presentation!

1 Fill a small stock pot with water and 1 teaspoon of salt. Boil and cook rice al dente (just like you would pasta) stirring once in a while. The water will not get all absorbed. Strain and transfer to a shallow pan to cool off.

2 Cut asparagus into 3-inch long pieces. Grate the orange zest in a bowl, then cut oranges in half and juice them into the bowl — stir well. Add the oil, salt and pepper. Add the scallops and let marinate for about 2 hours before using.

3 Preheat oven to 450°F.

4 Fold parchment paper in half so it is creased. Lay open and divide asparagus between all six on bottom half of the sheet. Divide scallops next. Top with ½ cup of the rice. Drizzle about 2 tablespoons of marinade on top. Fold over the parchment and secure the edges in the classic style, starting at one end and folding edge over edge around the open part. You could staple the two top corners if you wish.

5 Place all the "packages" on 2 baking sheets. Bake for 15–20 minutes. You will notice the parchment rise because of the steam and it will slightly color. When done take packages out of the oven and slide onto the serving plates. Tear open using scissors or your fingertips. Be careful of the steam! You can eat right from the "package."

WINE PAIRING '04 AJELLO "MAJUS"

1	cup olive oil
	all-purpose flour, for dredging
12	2 oz pieces sliced veal scaloppine
1½	lbs cleaned fresh baby artichokes, thinly sliced, (use canned if fresh are unavailable)
¾	lb ramps or leeks
	salt and pepper
	vegetable stock
1	cup Cinzano Vinaigrette (see page 177)

CARNE — SERVES 6

Scaloppine di Vitello con i Carciofi

VEAL SCALLOPS WITH SPRING VEGETABLES

1 Heat oil in large pan. Dredge meat in the flour and lay it in the hot oil. Cook 1 minute, and then turn the meat to the other side. Cook 1 more minute, then add artichokes and the ramps. Season with salt and pepper. Add a little vegetable stock to the pan if it is getting dry. Couple more minutes and its done!

FOR THE PRESENTATION

2 Serve 2 slices of veal, topped with the vegetables and drizzle with the vinaigrette.

WINE PAIRING '04 LA MOZZA MORELLINO DI SCANSANO

Experience Italy!

Every day, we eat and drink Italy at Paesano's. We offer classes on how to speak Italian and even teach customers how to properly order food in Italian. But perhaps our most authentic Italian experience is our annual guided tour of this most wonderful country that inspires our restaurant.

Each fall we select a region of Italy to explore and along with our good friends at Cultural Encounters, take an intimate group on an unforgettable Italian experience. Previous trips include Veneto, Sicilia, Toscana [Tuscany], Sorrento and the breathtaking Italian Riviera. Included in these guided tours are stops at major attractions as well as the private, less traveled stops. We visit wine estates, dine at the finest restaurants, stay at some of the world's foremost hotels and discover what makes each region so unique.

If there were an all-encompassing theme for these trips, it would be culture. From the olive gardens of Lake Garda, to the ruins of Pompeii, and to the Renaissance Masters of Florence, our group experiences many of the world's most treasured places. We also get a chance to visit some old friends like good friends Dario Boscaini from the Masi Winery and Luca Currado of Vietti. And, we always try to make it up to see Isabella's family in Trissino.

Due to the popularity of our excursions, we decided in 2006 to add a second trip in the spring centered around the infamous "VinItaly" Wine Expo, one of the world's largest exposition of fine wines. This trip takes us back to Veneto, Isabella's homeland and a region where we discover something new [and old] every time we visit.

These annual tours are truly an authentic Italian experience!

1 cup canned artichoke hearts, drained
1 cup pepperoncini peppers, stems off
1½ cups breadcrumbs
1 egg
2 lbs pork tenderloin
olive oil
12 thin slices provolone cheese

CARNE — SERVES 6

Filetto di Maiale in Crosta

PEPPERONCINI AND ARTICHOKE CRUSTED PORK TENDERLOIN

1 To prepare "crust" for tenderloin grind the artichokes and pepperoncini together in a food processor. Scrape it into a bowl. Add breadcrumbs and egg and mix well.

2 Trim excess fat from pork tenderloin and slice into 12 pieces on the bias. Lightly pound them between two sheets of plastic wrap to avoid "smashing" the meat. Cover each side of each slice of pork with about 1 oz of the "crust", spreading and pressing with your fingers to make sure most of the meat is covered.

3 Using a large pan, pour enough oil to cover the bottom and heat. Lay the slices of pork in the pan, whatever you can fit without crowding the pan, so they can sear. Cook each side for 2–3 minutes.

4 Take cooked slices of pork and place on sprayed oven tray. Cover them with the slices of provolone cheese. Turn the broiler to high and let the cheese melt. When melted, it is ready to serve.

FOR THE PRESENTATION

5 Serve with roasted potatoes and grilled asparagus. Lay the pork overlapping the slices next to the vegetables and garnish with a sprig of fresh herbs.

WINE PAIRING '04 CORDERO DI MONTEZEMOLO ARNEIS

- 1¼ cups heavy cream
- 5 tbsp powdered sugar
- 1 cup ricotta cheese
- ¼ cup whole pistachios, chopped
- ¼ cup chocolate, grated
- 1 lemon, zested
- 1 lime, zested
- 2 tbsp fresh ginger, puréed or minced

DOLCE — SERVES 4-6

Semifreddo di Ricotta allo Zenzero

GINGER RICOTTA SEMIFREDDO

1 Whip the heavy cream with the powdered sugar. Then, whip the ricotta separately for a couple minutes. Fold the cream into the ricotta and fold in the rest of the ingredients.

2 Serve in large wine glasses.

WINE PAIRING '04 BENI DI BATASIOLO MOSCATO D'ASTI "BOSC DLA REI"

DOLCE — YIELD 1 9-INCH PIE

Torta di Ricotta

ISABELLA'S RICOTTA PIE

For the Crust

1 cup graham cracker crumbs
2 tbsp sugar
4 tbsp unsalted butter

For the Garnish

½ cup raspberries
½ cup blueberries
½ cup strawberries
1 tbsp sugar
mint, optional

For the Filling

2 gelatin sheets
1½ cup ricotta cheese
4 tbsp honey
1 cup heavy cream, whipped

FOR THE CRUST

1 Melt the butter with the sugar and remove from the stove. Combine with the graham cracker crumbs. Put in pan pressing crumbs into it to form the crust.

FOR THE FILLING

2 Soften the gelatin sheets in a pan in about 1 inch of cold water.

3 Combine the ricotta cheese and honey in a bowl. Fold in the whipped cream.

4 Remove the gelatin sheets from the water, squeezing out excess water, and heat in a small pan over low heat until gelatin melts without boiling.

5 Fold the gelatin into the cheese mixture, a little at a time to get it distributed evenly.

6 Pour over the crust, spreading evenly, and let chill for at least 3 hours.

7 Combine berries and sugar and let sit to release some juice.

8 Slice pie, pour over some berries and garnish with some mint, if available.

WINE PAIRINGS '04 BENI DI BATASIDO MOSCATO D'ASTI "BOSC DLA REI"

LIQUORE VOV CREMA DI UOVA

For the Filling

5 lemons
2 cups sugar
4 eggs

For the Crust

1¼ cups all-purpose flour
10 tbsp unsalted butter, chilled and cut in small pieces
3 tbsp sugar
2 tbsp milk

DOLCE — YIELD 1 9-INCH PIE

Crostata al Limone

LEMON PIE

FOR THE FILLING

1 Peel and section the lemons, removing all the seeds as you go. Add the sugar to the pieces.

2 In another bowl whisk the eggs. Later, when you are ready to fill the pie, add the eggs to the lemons and sugar and mix well.

FOR THE CRUST

3 In the food processor, combine all the ingredients to make a dough. Roll the dough out in 2 pieces, for the top and bottom of pie. Fit one piece into the bottom of a pie pan, add the filling then cover with the second piece of dough, sealing the two together and trimming any excess dough.

4 Brush the crust with milk. Bake at 350°F for just under an hour until the crust is golden. Let sit before cutting to allow filling to set.

LIQUORE MASI GRAPPA DI RECIOTO DI AMARONE

For Tart Shell

1 cup plus 2 tbsp all-purpose flour
¼ cup yellow cornmeal
¼ cup sugar
½ tsp baking powder
pinch of salt
7 tbsp butter, chilled, cut in pieces
1 egg
1 egg yolk

For the Filling

2 eggs
2 yolks
¾ cup sugar
2 lemons
½ cup lemon juice
3½ oz butter, room temperature

DOLCE — YIELDS 1 9-INCH TART OR 10-12 4-INCH PIES

Crostata di Limone con Farina di Polenta

CORNMEAL CRUSTED LEMON TART

People! More polenta for you! Sweet though, in a dessert.

FOR TART SHELL

1 Combine the first 6 ingredients in a large bowl, and in batches, mix in food processor to make an even, crumbly dough.

2 Whisk together the eggs and yolks and gradually add them to the dough, working it with your hands until it starts to come together. Don't worry if it seems too dry; it takes a little while for the semolina to absorb the moisture. Roll dough out between 2 sheets of plastic to about ¼-inch thickness.

3 Using the tart pan as a guide cut out circles of dough to fit the pan (or pans). Chill dough.

4 To bake the shell, cut out squares (small, if using 4-inch pans) of paper and set in shell, then weigh down with dry rice or dry beans. Bake at 350°F until colored at the edges, about 20 minutes. Remove from oven and take out the weight. Bake again for a few minutes longer until the bottoms are cooked. Let shell cool.

FOR THE FILLING

5 In a large bowl whisk the eggs, yolks, sugar, zest of the 2 lemons and the lemon juice. Over a double boiler, cook this mixture stirring it constantly with a wooden spoon until it thickens and coats the back of a spoon. Be careful not to boil and scramble the eggs.

6 Remove from the heat and whisk in the butter until it is all incorporated. Pour into shell and refrigerate until set.

7 When chilled, pie is ready to be enjoyed!

LIQUORE PALLINI LIMONCELLO

Summer is about colors, light food and trips to the market. At the summer markets farmers offer the best of their products — the peppers and tomatoes, the herbs, the nice lettuce, it is all there! For sure, you don't have to think about what to do for lunch or dinner. It is easy to make a quick pasta salad, throw something on the grill and enjoy some gelato!

Sagre [or fairs] are a big summer deal all over Italy — mostly on the weekends. Lots of people come out in the small villages and set up tents in local fields. There is music and dancing and tables full of food! The air is filled with the smell of grilling — sausages, pork ribs and salami. You can be sure to find wine and beer, just a great time!

estate

SUMMER

4	3 oz pieces center cut Ahi-tuna loin
2	eggs
1	cup flour
1	cup breadcrumbs
2	tbsp extra virgin olive oil
½	cup prosciutto
1	cup spinach, fresh
4	tbsp pine nuts
	Balsamic Glaze, for drizzling (see page 176)
	salt and pepper
¼	cup oil for pan frying the tuna

ANTIPASTO — SERVES 4

Tonno Impanato

BREADED GLAZED AHI TUNA WITH WILTED SPINACH, PROSCIUTTO AND PINE NUTS

FOR THE PREPARATION

1 Place eggs, flour and breadcrumbs in 3 separate bowls.

2 Dredge the tuna pieces first into the flour, then the eggs and lastly the breadcrumbs, coating well with each step.

3 Heat oil in pan and cook tuna until golden on each side. If you like your tuna rare, just keep it on the side until you've prepared the toppings. Otherwise you can place it in a pre-heated 450°F oven for about 5-6 minutes, which will cook the fish more completely.

FOR THE TOPPINGS

4 Heat extra virgin olive oil in pan. Add prosciutto and let it get crispy. Add spinach and cook until wilted. Then, add pine nuts. Season with salt and pepper.

FOR THE PRESENTATION

5 Serve the toppings on top of the tuna, and then drizzle with the Balsamic Glaze.

WINE PAIRING '01 SCHIOPETTO "BLANC DES ROSIS"

For the Procedure

1½ cups assorted Grilled Vegetables, cut into small strips (see page 67)
½ cup Lemon-Thyme Dressing (see recipe below)
4 Tortino al Couscous (see page 68)
2 heads Belgian endive, cut into very thin strips (reserve 12 external leaves for garnish)

For the Lemon Thyme Dressing

1 tbsp fresh thyme, chopped
juice of 1 lemon
pinch of salt and ground black pepper
1½ cups mayonnaise
¾ cups buttermilk

INSALATA — SERVES 4

Insalata di Verdure

SEASONAL GRILLED VEGETABLE SALAD

In Italy, a salad is just mixed greens, with an occasional tomato, radish and shredded carrots. We serve it as a side, unlike in America, where people often make it a meal. So I have added to the traditional and created some very tasty salads that our customers really enjoy.

FOR THE LEMON THYME DRESSING

1 Combine all the ingredients and mix well. Refrigerate.

FOR THE PROCEDURE

2 Place grilled vegetables and endive strips in bowl. Add dressing and mix well.

FOR THE PRESENTATION

3 Divide the contents of the bowl onto 4 large plates. Insert 3 endive leaves for decoration and let them extend out from under the mound of salad. Place a warm Tortino al Couscous on the side of the plate.

4 Ready to serve!

WINE PAIRING '04 REGALEALI ROSATO

8 cups water
1 cup white vinegar
2 tsp salt
3 Yukon gold potatoes, washed, skin on, thinly sliced
2 zucchini, thinly sliced
3 tbsp butter
6 oz (¾ cup) Gorgonzola cheese, grated
oil for frying
all-purpose flour, for dredging

ANTIPASTO — SERVES 4

Chips di Patate e Zucchini

ZUCCHINI AND POTATO CHIPS

Summertime in Italy is when people just enjoy being outside, going to the park, and being with friends. Always you see people stopping for an aperitif before going home for lunch. Typically, Italians might order a Gingerino, similar to bitters that are served in America. Mixed with wine or juice, the snack of choice is potato chips. Here, I've used "real" potatoes and zucchini, and sliced them thinly to make "homemade" chips and topped it all with Gorgonzola cheese. This is wonderful!

A mandoline would be the perfect tool for this recipe unless you have great cutting skills for thinly slicing the vegetables.

FOR THE POTATOES

1 Place first 3 ingredients in a pot and bring to a boil.

2 Add potatoes to the water and let sit 1–2 minutes. Drain, let cool and keep in cold water until ready to use.

FOR THE PREPARATION

3 Prepare large pan with frying oil and heat to about 375°F.

4 Flour the zucchini by placing in a large bowl and tossing well with flour. Transfer zucchini to a fine strainer and gently shake to remove excess flour.

5 Deep-fry a few at a time until they turn a nice golden color. Remove from oil and drain on paper towel. Place on tray.

6 Drain potatoes from water and pat dry. Deep-fry them a few at a time until golden in color. Drain on paper towel and place on tray with zucchini.

7 In a small pan melt the butter until it starts to sizzle. Add Gorgonzola cheese and stir with a spoon making sure it melts without burning the bottom of the pan. It will separate because of the high fat content, so add 2 tablespoons of water to it and stir quickly.

FOR THE PRESENTATION

8 Divide the chips onto 4 dishes or keep it all on 1 platter. Pour melted cheese over all the chips.

WINE PAIRING '04 PALAMA SALENTO ROSATO "ALBAROSSA"

½	cup extra virgin olive oil
2	lbs fresh mussels (about 4 dozen), washed and de-bearded
6	shallots, peeled and quartered
1	sprig fresh thyme
2	bay leaves
2	sprigs flat parsley
1	cup white wine
½	tsp saffron threads
	salt and pepper
8	small slices sourdough bread

ANTIPASTO — SERVES 4

Cozze con lo Zafferano

MUSSELS WITH SAFFRON

1 Heat oil in a pan and add the cleaned mussels. Let them cook for a few minutes keeping the pan covered.

2 Add the shallots, herbs, saffron, seasonings and wine. The mussels are done when they open up.

3 Take the mussels out of the pan and arrange in a serving bowl.

FOR THE PRESENTATION

4 Taste the sauce and season with salt and pepper. Don't be afraid of salt. It brings food to life! Pour it over the mussels. Serve with slices of grilled bread on the side.

WINE PAIRING '01 CAPARZO "LE GRANCE"

ANTIPASTO — SERVES 4

Gamberi al Forno

OVEN ROASTED SHRIMP WITH SWEET PEPPER SALSA

For the Shrimp Breading

1 cup breadcrumbs
½ cup Parmigiano Reggiano cheese
1 tbsp fresh thyme, chopped
1 tbsp fresh basil, chopped
pinch of salt and pepper

For the Procedure

16 shrimp, peeled and deveined
extra virgin olive oil
radicchio, for garnish
Sweet Pepper Salsa (see recipe below)

For the Sweet Pepper Salsa

4 tbsp red wine vinegar
½ cup sugar
1 red pepper, seeded and chopped small dice
1 yellow pepper, seeded and chopped small dice
2 Roma tomatoes, seeded and chopped small dice
1 tbsp garlic, chopped
2 tbsp red onion, minced
1 tbsp fresh basil, chopped
salt and pepper

FOR THE SHRIMP BREADING

1 Mix all ingredients together and refrigerate until ready to use.

FOR THE PROCEDURE

2 Butterfly shrimp (see page 14) and lightly coat them with oil, then dip in breading mixture and bread each side of the shrimp pressing down to get a nice, secure coat.

3 Preheat oven to 450°F. Place shrimp on baking sheet and bake for 12–15 minutes.

FOR THE SWEET PEPPER SALSA

4 In a small pot, boil the vinegar and sugar. Remove from heat.

5 Combine peppers and tomatoes. Add rest of ingredients and the vinegar mixture. Mix well.

6 Store in a container and let sit for a few hours to blend flavors.

FOR THE PRESENTATION

7 Arrange shrimp on 4 small plates, garnishing with radicchio. Place 2–3 tablespoons of Sweet Pepper Salsa on plate and drizzle with olive oil.

WINE PAIRING '04 MASO CANALI PINOT GRIGIO

For the Procedure

- 4 tbsp butter
- ½ bunch asparagus, ends removed and thinly sliced
- Preserved Lemon (see recipe below)
- 2 tbsp Basil Coulis (see recipe below)
- 2 tbsp Lemon Marmalade (see recipe below)
- 32 mozzarella balls, cherry size
- salt and pepper
- sprig of basil

For the Basil Coulis

- ¼ cup packed fresh basil leaves, finely chopped
- ½ cup olive oil

For the Preserved Lemon

- 1 lemon, large, washed and sliced thinly (12 slices)
- ½ cup water
- 1 cup sugar

For the Lemon Marmalade

- 4 lemons
- ¼ cup sugar
- 2 tbsp extra virgin olive oil
- pinch of salt
- pinch of ground black pepper

ANTIPASTO — SERVES 4

Bocconcini con Asparagi

FRESH MOZZARELLA BALLS WITH ASPARAGUS

Asparagus is the vegetable that seems to scream "spring has arrived!" A big tradition back home is to eat "Asparagi lessi con le uova," boiled eggs and asparagus the day after Easter, on Pasquetta, Little Easter. I never was a big fan of it, but now after many years away from my family, I like to keep the tradition going in a different country.

You need to prepare the Preserved Lemon, Basil Coulis, and Lemon Marmalade the day before making this recipe. Any leftovers can be frozen for future use.

FOR THE PROCEDURE

1 Heat butter in a large pan, add asparagus and cook for 1 minute. Add Preserved Lemon with the juice, the Basil Coulis and Lemon Marmalade. Bring it to a boil.

2 Add fresh mozzarella and let it warm up in the pan until you see it start to get slightly soft. Season with salt and pepper.

FOR THE BASIL COULIS

3 Place chopped basil in tall cup and add oil. Using a blender, food processor or hand immersion tool, blend the mixture. Place in a small container and refrigerate until ready to use.

FOR THE PRESERVED LEMON

4 In a small pot bring water and sugar to a boil. Remove from heat and add lemon slices. Cover and let sit overnight before using.

FOR THE LEMON MARMALADE

5 Zest all the lemons and dice the fruit in small cubes. Do not use any of the white part!

6 Combine the lemons and zest in a saucepan with the remaining ingredients. Heat until the mixture begins to bubble. Cook slowly for about 10 minutes. Stir well and make sure the sugar is all dissolved. Cool before serving.

FOR THE PRESENTATION

7 Arrange the cheese into 4 soup bowls, and then equally distribute the juice. Garnish with a sprig of basil and serve.

WINE PAIRING '04 MASSONE GAVI

¾ cup garbanzo beans or 1 can, drained
¼ cup goat cheese
1 egg
¼ cup bread flour
2 tbsp whole milk
pinch of salt and ground pepper
oil for frying

ANTIPASTO — YIELDS 30-40 FRITTERS

Ceci in Pastella Fritti

CHICKPEA FRITTERS

You know what I love to eat in the summer? Zucchini flowers! When I go back home each August, my mamma goes crazy trying to find some zucchini flowers. She "coats" them in a batter, simply deep fries them and sprinkles them with salt. Sooo tasty, I can eat 20-30 at a time. These chickpea fritters are another very good summer snack!

If you don't have a fryer thermometer, drop a piece of dry bread in the oil. It will start to get all "bubbly" around the bread if the oil has reached the right temperature.

1 Purée the beans and combine with remaining ingredients. Mix well.

2 Heat frying oil in pan to 375°F. Using a spoon or small ice cream scoop, drop the batter in the oil and let it fry until it becomes a nice deep gold color all around.

3 Drain on paper towel. Serve on a platter.

WINE PAIRING '03 VIETTI DOLCETTO D'ALBA "TRE VIGNE"

12 small slices sourdough bread, ½-inch thick
2–3 garlic cloves, peeled
4 Breaded Shrimp, baked (see page 59)
8 tbsp Sweet Pepper Salsa (see page 59)
1 cup Grilled Vegetables, assorted, cut in strips (see page 67)
1 cup tomatoes, small dice
8 thin slices fresh mozzarella
4 fresh basil leaf, chopped
salt and pepper
extra virgin olive oil

ANTIPASTO — YIELDS 12 PIECES ASSORTED BRUSCHETTA

Trio di Bruschetta

ISABELLA'S SUMMER ITALIAN TOASTS

And of course, bruschetta! Since people go nuts for bruschetta you will see that I have it listed in the summer section as well as fall in the cookbook. It truly is not tied to any season and is eaten year-round. In Italy, we have restaurants that serve only bruschetta, they are called bruschetterie. You are served a large slice of toasted bread, and 90% of the time it is rubbed with garlic, then sliced into smaller portions with your choice of many, many toppings. Grab a beer or sip your wine. Che gusto!

1 Toast bread in oven until it gets a golden color. Rub the garlic all over the bread, both sides.

2 Season tomatoes with basil, salt and pepper.

FOR THE PRESENTATION

3 Top 4 slices of the bread with the grilled vegetables, 4 with the seasoned tomatoes and mozzarella, and 4 with the Sweet Pepper Salsa and Breaded Shrimp. Place 1 of each on 4 plates and drizzle all with extra virgin olive oil.

WINE PAIRING NV NINO FRANCO PROSECCO "RUSTICO"

For the Procedure

8 bamboo skewers (4-6 inches long)
24 cherry tomatoes
24 mozzarella balls, cherry size
fresh basil
extra virgin olive oil
salt and pepper
½ cup Basil Vinaigrette (see recipe below)

For the Basil Vinaigrette

1 cup fresh basil, packed full
2 tbsp lemon juice
1 tsp sherry wine vinegar
1 tbsp Dijon mustard
½ cup extra virgin olive oil

INSALATA — SERVES 4

Insalata Caprese

CAPRESE SALAD SKEWERS WITH BASIL VINAIGRETTE

Though Caprese salad is not typical for the Veneto region, it is well known throughout Italy. Here, I've put my own "twist" on the classic dish.

FOR THE PROCEDURE

1 Soak the skewers in water for about 30 minutes to keep them from burning later on the grill.

2 Alternately skewer 1 cherry tomato and 1 fresh mozzarella ball using 3 of each per skewer. Place 2 fresh basil leaves between each tomato and cheese pair. Lay the skewers on a tray and lightly drizzle both sides with olive oil, salt and pepper.

3 Make sure the grill is very hot. Lay out the skewers on the grill. Keep turning them to keep the mozzarella from melting off the skewers. Grill for about 2-3 minutes.

FOR THE BASIL VINAIGRETTE

4 Clean and de-stem the basil. Place leaves into a food processor with the lemon juice, sherry wine vinegar, and the Dijon mustard. Pulse the mixture until the basil is chopped well. Leaving the food processor running, slowly drizzle in the oil.

FOR THE PRESENTATION

5 Place the skewers on a serving tray drizzled with the Basil Vinaigrette.

WINE PAIRING '04 VALDINERA ROERO ARNEIS

16 slices pancetta, thinly sliced
5 cups mixed greens
salt and pepper
1 red tomato, large, sliced into 4 slices
1 yellow tomato, large, sliced into 4 slices
1 green tomato, large, sliced into 4 slices
4 tbsp Balsamic Glaze (see page 176)
extra virgin olive oil

INSALATA — SERVES 4

Insalata con Pancetta e Pomodori Assortiti

PANCETTA BACON & COLORFUL SUMMER TOMATO SALAD

Ah, la pancetta! Love it, as I love all pork meat. Sometimes all we had for dinner was sautéed pancetta, polenta and mixed greens. Of course, always red wine on the table too!

1 Place pancetta on baking tray in preheated oven at 350°F. Bake until almost crispy.

FOR THE PRESENTATION

2 Place some of the mixed greens on each plate. Season lightly with salt, pepper and a little extra virgin olive oil. Lay one slice of red tomato on each plate, top with pancetta and just keep alternating until you run out of ingredients. Finish the dish by drizzling the salad with the Balsamic Glaze.

WINE PAIRING '04 ROSA DEL GOLFO SALENTO ROSATO

1 zucchini
1 yellow squash
1 eggplant
2 large tomatoes
2 red peppers
2 yellow peppers
3 tbsp fresh oregano, chopped
salt and pepper
extra virgin olive oil
Venetian Breaded Rice Balls (see page 69)

ANTIPASTO — SERVES 4

Verdure alla Griglia & Arancini di Riso

GRILLED VEGETABLE PLATTER & VENETIAN BREADED RICE BALLS

You could go crazy at the Italian market during the summer months! There are so many vegetables to choose from — you can't go wrong no matter what you choose.

1 Cut squashes and eggplant into ⅛-inch slices lengthwise and cut tomato into ½-inch slices. Season all with salt and pepper and drizzle with olive oil.

2 Get the grill hot and begin grilling peppers whole, turning them as they begin to char. When all sides are charred place them in a paper bag. Once they have cooled remove them from the bag, peel skin off, open them and remove seeds. Slice and place on large platter.

3 Keep grilling all the other vegetables, making sure to give some nice black char marks on both sides of the slice.

FOR THE PRESENTATION

4 Add vegetables to the large platter as you remove them from the grill. Season with salt and pepper. Sprinkle them with the chopped oregano and drizzle a little more extra virgin olive oil over them. Serve with Venetian Breaded Rice Balls.

WINE PAIRING '04 MORIS FARMS VERMENTINO

½ lb couscous
1½ tbsp butter
6 tbsp Parmigiano Reggiano cheese
pinch of salt
all-purpose flour, for dredging
oil for frying

Non so perché ci vestivano sempre con i vestiti uguali!

CONTORNO — SERVES 4

Tortino al Couscous

COUSCOUS CAKE

1 Prepare couscous according to directions on box. When cooked, place in mixing bowl and stir in the butter and cheese. Let sit for a few minutes.

2 Line a tray or small baking sheet with parchment paper.

3 Using a small lid or a small cookie cutter (about 3 inches in diameter and 1½ inches deep) form small discs of couscous, making sure they are pretty dense. Refrigerate until cold.

4 Heat frying oil in pan. Flour the "cakes" on both sides and sear them until you obtain a nice golden color all over. Keep them warm in the oven until the salad is ready to serve.

For the Rice Balls

4 tbsp vegetable bouillon
½ lb Arborio rice
½ onion, peeled, chopped
2 tbsp olive oil
½ cup Parmigiano Reggiano cheese
2 tbsp unsalted butter

Breading Procedure

2 cups bread flour
pinch of salt and pepper
4 eggs
3 cups breadcrumbs

CONTORNO — SERVES 4

Arancini di Riso

VENETIAN BREADED RICE BALLS

FOR THE RICE BALLS

1 Put a quart of water in a stockpot and bring to a boil adding vegetable bouillon unless you have vegetable stock available.

2 Warm up another pot and add oil. Sauté onion.

3 Cook the rice as you would for any risotto, following the procedure described in the recipe for Balsamic and Parmesan Risotto Cakes on page 146.

4 After cooking, spread the rice out on a large sheet pan and put it into the refrigerator to cool. When cool, scoop out the rice using an ice cream scoop. Bread the balls using the standard breading procedure.

BREADING PROCEDURE

5 Place the flour in a bowl and season with the salt and pepper.

6 Crack and whip the eggs in another bowl. Sift the breadcrumbs in a third bowl.

7 Place one or two rice balls into the flour at a time. Dip one at a time in the eggs. Drip off excess egg and place balls in the breadcrumbs. Brush some breadcrumbs over to cover, carefully pressing down with your hand, to ensure that the breadcrumbs will stick in an even coating.

8 Remove from the breadcrumbs and shake off any excess breading. Place on a sheet tray covered with parchment paper. Deep-fry when needed.

- 2 zucchini
- 1 eggplant, peeled
- 4 tbsp extra virgin olive oil
- salt and pepper
- 1 lb cappellini pasta, uncooked
- 6 oz (¾ cup) sun-dried tomatoes, julienned*
- ½ cup fresh ricotta

PASTA — SERVES 4

Pasta Veronese

VERONA STYLE SUMMER PASTA

A nice and easy dish to prepare all summer long! Japanese eggplant is best for this preparation because it is firmer than regular eggplant.

The spiral slicer tool is available at www.famousfood.com.

1 Cut the zucchini and eggplant into very thin strips. The strips should look almost as thin as the cappellini. Use the spiral slicer tool, if you have one, or a julienne slicer. Set aside.

2 Heat a large sauté pan on the stove with olive oil. Add zucchini and eggplant at the same time. They will cook quickly because they are cut so thin. Season lightly with salt and pepper. Stir the vegetables with a wooden spoon. Add the tomatoes that have been cut into small pieces.

3 At this point, turn off the stove. Bring a large pot of water to a boil. Add a little salt to the water and cook the pasta until al dente according to the package directions.

4 Drain the pasta and reserve a little water just in case you'll need it to add to the pan.

5 Turn the heat back on the vegetables and add the pasta to them. Toss it until it is well mixed.

6 If desired, add olive oil from the jar of marinated tomatoes. Stir in the ricotta cheese.

FOR THE PRESENTATION

1 Divide pasta onto 4 plates and garnish with any extra toppings.

**Put sun-dried tomatoes in a jar with 3 oz of olive oil, 1 tsp chopped garlic and 1 tbsp of fresh basil. Let rest at least overnight before using.*

WINE PAIRING '03 LE CASELLE CHIANTI

For the Crespelle Batter, Yields 15–20 crespelle

- 3 eggs
- 1 cup (8 oz) bread flour
- 2½ cups whole milk
- pinch of salt
- 1 tbsp olive oil

For the Crespelle Filling

- 1½ lb fresh ricotta cheese
- 1 cup Parmigiano Reggiano cheese
- 1 egg
- ½–1 tsp salt
- ½ tsp pepper
- 4 tbsp Parmigiano Reggiano cheese, to top crespelle

PASTA — SERVES 4

Crespelle di Ricotta

RICOTTA FILLED CREPES WITH SUMMER VEGETABLE STEW

This wonderful cheesy dish takes some organization, but don't be afraid! Some of it can be prepared ahead, then assembled another day. I am a big fan of crespelle because they are just so much fun and you can do so much with them. They are often associated with a cheese filling and that is what I have done here - surprise! No twist on the traditional!

FOR THE CRESPELLE BATTER

1 Crack the eggs into a bowl. Whisk together the eggs and flour, then gradually add the milk. Continue to stir to prevent lumps. Pass through a strainer to obtain a nice and smooth batter.

2 Put the batter back in a bowl and add salt and oil. Let it rest for a few minutes.

3 Get 1 omelet pan (or two if you have enough skills!). Get it hot on the stove and spray with pan spray. Using a small ladle (2 oz) get some of the batter (but don't fill the ladle all the way up) and pour it into the pan rotating it at the same time to get the batter all over the bottom of the pan. Put back on the stove and cook for 10-15 seconds. Flip the crespelle on the other side and let cook for another 10-15 seconds.

4 Lay on a tray or baking sheet until all the batter is used. Stack crespelle on top of each other. Wrap in plastic wrap and refrigerate.

5 May be refrigerated for up to 1 week or frozen for up to 3 weeks.

FOR THE CRESPELLE FILLING

6 Mix all the ingredients together, except cheese topping and store them in the refrigerator until you are ready to use.

For the Procedure

8 Crespelle, stuffed
4 tbsp melted butter
4 tbsp Parmigiano Reggiano cheese
Summer Vegetable Stew
Crespelle Filling (see previous page)

For Summer Vegetable Stew

4 tbsp extra virgin olive oil
½ cup red onions, small dice
2 Roma tomatoes, chopped
vegetable stock, store bought or homemade
8 oz green patty pan squash or 1 green and 1 yellow zucchini, cut into 1-inch dice
6 oz rapini greens
salt and pepper
4 tbsp Parmigiano Reggiano cheese

FOR THE PROCEDURE

7 Lay the crepes on the table. Using a pastry bag filled with the ricotta filling mix, squeeze out about ⅓ cup in each crepe. The mixture can be easily spread as well.

8 Roll up the crespelle and place on baking sheet. Brush with melted butter and sprinkle with cheese. Bake in 450°F preheated oven for about 30 minutes. While the crespelle are baking, prepare the Summer Vegetable Stew.

FOR SUMMER VEGETABLE STEW

9 Warm the oil in a pan. Add onions and tomatoes. Let cook for a few minutes. Add the squash and keep cooking for 3–4 minutes then add about ½ cup of the vegetable stock. Season with salt and pepper. Add the rapini greens and let cook until wilted.

FOR THE PRESENTATION

10 Pour the stew into 4 pasta bowls. Top with 2 crisscrossed crespelle and drizzle with a little extra virgin olive oil and the cheese.

WINE PAIRING '04 DONNAFUGATA "ANTHILIA"

Formaggio

I love cheese!

When I was little, I used to go, more with my papá than my mamma, to the market. They were always giving to me some piece of cheese to taste [very good!] while my papá was shopping.

The latteria, the small cheese store in Trissino, had this great smell of dairy [I can still remember it]. And still today, when I go back home I take a quick visit to it for a small piece of Asiago.

Grana Padano is the cheese that my family uses the most. I actually prefer that one to the world known Parmigiano Reggiano because of its texture and sweetness. So, just because the recipes call for Parmigiano Reggiano, it doesn't mean that you cannot use Grana Padano or the recipes would be less good! Remember, the real Grana Padano, the real Italian thing, is definitely the best choice; any surrogate I guess it would be okay, but you won't have my blessing!

1 tbsp extra virgin olive oil
1 medium size onion, thinly sliced
6 oz pancetta, cut into strips
½ cup white wine
1½ lbs fresh cherry tomatoes, cut in half
1 tsp freshly ground black pepper
1 tbsp red pepper flakes
1 lb bucatini or penne rigate pasta, uncooked
Pecorino Romano cheese, freshly grated

PASTA — SERVES 4-6

Pasta all' Amatriciana

SPICY PASTA WITH PANCETTA BACON

Not from the Veneto but... man, this dish is good! "Amatriciana" means that the recipe comes from the city of Amatrice. Pancetta or bacon is always one of the ingredients. Typically, it is served with a bucatini noodle, a thick hollow spaghetti pasta. The penne rigate, though shorter, is much the same and is fine to use.

1 Heat the oil in a 10-inch skillet. Add the onions and cook, stirring until they are translucent, about 5-8 minutes. Add the pancetta and cook briefly, stirring, until it releases its flavor, about 5-8 minutes.

2 Add the wine and let it evaporate for a minute. Stir in the tomatoes, freshly ground black pepper and the pepper flakes. Bring the sauce to a boil and reduce the heat to low simmer. Cook for about 10-15 minutes.

3 Meanwhile, bring a large pot of water to a boil. Add a little salt to the boiling water and cook the pasta until al-dente, according to the package directions.

FOR THE PRESENTATION

4 Drain and toss the pasta with the sauce and divide onto plates. Top with freshly grated Pecorino Romano cheese.

WINE PAIRING '02 VESEVO AGLIANICO BENEVENTANO

28–30 pieces of ravioli (store bought vegetable stuffed, spinach-ricotta, or cheese)
1 cup Beurre Blanc (see recipe below)
12 Breaded Shrimp (see page 59)
½ cup Parmigiano Reggiano cheese, shaved

For the Beurre Blanc
2 cups white wine
1 shallot, peeled, thinly sliced
½ cup heavy cream
8 tbsp butter, cut into small pieces
pinch of salt
1 tbsp fresh thyme, chopped

PASTA — SERVES 4

Ravioli di Verdure

VEGETABLE STUFFED RAVIOLI WITH THYME FLAVORED BEURRE BLANC AND OVEN ROASTED SHRIMP WITH PARMESAN CHEESE CURLS

Ravioli and tortellini are very popular items on Italian menus. The classic tortellini is filled with meat, though you will see both ravioli and tortellini with meat and cheese fillings. Ravioli allow a little more room for the filling and a little less pasta, so I tend to use it more often. The sauce will take some time to prepare so for me, I would get it ready the day before. Then, all you have to do is warm it up.

FOR THE BEURRE BLANC

1 In a pot, add shallots to the wine and let boil until mixture reduces almost by half.

2 In a separate pot, reduce the cream by half. Strain wine from the shallots. Add cream to the wine. Bring it to a boil and reduce by half again. Season with salt and thyme. Using a whisk, incorporate the butter little by little. Store until ready to use.

3 Cook the ravioli according to directions on package and prepare shrimp as directed in recipe on page 59.

FOR THE PRESENTATION

4 Heat the sauce in a large pan and add the drained ravioli. Toss them until well coated. Divide and place in 4 bowls, topping each with the shrimp. Sprinkle cheese on top and enjoy!

WINE PAIRING '03 FEUDI DI SAN GREGORIO FIANO D'AVELLINO

6 tbsp olive oil
3 dozen mussels, washed and de-bearded
½ cup prosciutto, cut into small strips
4 tbsp breadcrumbs and 4 tablespoons grated Parmigiano Reggiano, toasted and mixed together
1 cup Preserved Lemons, with syrup (see page 61)
Potato Dumplings, (see page 150)
salt and pepper

PASTA — SERVES 4

Gnocchi di Patate con le Cozze

POTATO DUMPLINGS WITH MUSSELS

Making gnocchi is "laborioso" [labor intense] and is better to make in the fall or winter when you don't want to be outside freezing your buns off. But, my mamma makes it in the summer during those rainy days when you cannot do much outside. I grew up eating gnocchi just with tomato sauce, sugar and cinnamon. I still eat it that way today.

1 Heat oil in a large pan. Add mussels and cover with a lid until they start to open. Add prosciutto and stir it once in a while to get crispy.

2 Add the lemons and the syrup and bring them to a light boil, then simmer. At this point, cook the gnocchi, then add them to the sauce and mix the ingredients all together.

FOR THE PRESENTATION

3 Serve the dish on a platter, keeping the gnocchi in the middle and the mussels on the outside. Sprinkle with the breadcrumb mix, previously toasted for a few minutes in a pan.

WINE PAIRING '03 FATTORI SOAVE

Adoravo quel vestito!

For the Procedure

8 3 oz pork loin slices, ½-inch thick and lightly pounded
½ cup Cherry Chutney (see recipe below)
½ cup Apple-Basil Sauce (see recipe below)
4 Crespelle (see page 72)

For the Apple-Basil Sauce

2 Granny Smith apples, peeled and cored
juice from 1 lemon
¼ cup granulated sugar
4 tbsp fresh basil, finely chopped

For the Cherry Chutney

2 tbsp red onions, small dice
2 tbsp extra virgin olive oil
1 lb fresh cherries, pitted
½ cup brown sugar
2 tbsp lemon juice
¼ cup raisins
1 tbsp fresh mint, chopped

CARNE — SERVES 4

Maiale alla Griglia

GRILLED PORK LOIN WITH CHERRY CHUTNEY AND APPLE BASIL SAUCE

FOR THE PROCEDURE

1 Grill pork loin until fully cooked.

FOR THE APPLE-BASIL SAUCE

2 Cut apples into small pieces. Add lemon juice and sugar to apples. Using a food processor mix the ingredients to achieve a slushy consistency. Add the basil. Put into a container and refrigerate.

FOR THE CHERRY CHUTNEY

3 Cook the onion in the oil until translucent. Add the cherries, sugar and lemon juice. Cook for about 10 minutes or until the sauce starts to get juicy. Use an immersion blender to chop up the sauce until it's more of a "chutney" consistency. Return the mixture to the stove and bring it to a boil. Add the raisins and the mint. Simmer for a few more minutes. Store in the refrigerator. May also be frozen in small quantities for later use.

FOR THE PRESENTATION

4 On each plate lay 2 slices of pork, covering one with a dollop of Cherry Chutney and the other with Apple-Basil Sauce. Serve Crespelle as a side.

WINE PAIRING '04 CANTINE DEL NOTAIO AGLIANICO ROSATO "IL ROGITO"

- 4 single bone-in chicken breast with wing attached (or split 2 chicken fronts in half)
- 4 pork sausage
- Summer Vegetable Stew (see page 73)
- 1 tbsp fresh rosemary, chopped
- 1 tbsp fresh parsley, chopped
- 1 tbsp fresh basil, chopped
- 1 tsp garlic, chopped
- ½ cup olive oil
- ¾ cup olive oil
- salt and pepper

CARNE — SERVES 4

Pollo e Salsiccia

ROASTED BONE-IN CHICKEN BREAST WITH GRILLED PORK SAUSAGE & VEGETABLE STEW

For sure, Salsiccia is my favorite meat. The sausage you find in the Veneto are sweet and simply seasoned only with salt and pepper. They are best when they are grilled. Semplice e buona! The sausages you find at stores here in America are more what you find in Southern Italy, not quite as sweet and filled with fennel.

1 Combine the herbs, garlic and ½ cup oil in a bowl. Add the chicken and toss it to get it well coated. If possible, have it rest overnight for more flavor.

2 Preheat oven to 500°F.

3 Heat sauté pan on stove. Add olive oil.

4 Sear the chicken skin side down first, until it gets nice and crispy. Turn it on the other side and let it cook for another 2–3 minutes. Season with salt and pepper. Put the chicken on a baking sheet skin side up. Place in oven for about 20–30 minutes.

5 Meanwhile grill the sausage and when it is done, take off the heat and cover with foil. When cool enough to handle, cut on bias.

6 Prepare the Summer Vegetable Stew. When complete add sausage.

FOR THE PRESENTATION

7 Serve the stew on the bottom of the plate, placing chicken on top of it.

WINE PAIRING '02 IL MOLINO DI GRACE SANGIOVESE "IL VOLANO"

That's Italian

We tend to take the words "authentic Italian" seriously at Paesano's. Isabella has her signature on everything coming out of the kitchen. Beyond our food and award-winning Italian wine list, we offer a variety of ways to experience true Italian culture.

Every fall, we entertain a group of travelers for a guided tour of Italy. Each year, we select a different region to explore and sample the sights, foods and wines indigenous to that region. For anyone partaking in our excursions or planning a trip for themselves, we offer our "Italian 101" sessions, a special evening learning proper Italian etiquette while ordering and dining Italian style. Isabella and Chaad host the event held monthly, complete with dinner and matching wines.

Paesano's regular and Sicilian born [which Isabella doesn't hold against him], Signore Salvatore Bisaccia has built a strong following with his popular series of Italian language classes, offering three different levels of ability, three times per year. We also give our guests the opportunity to celebrate a cherished bottle of wine with friends. We call it "that special bottle" night and Wine Director Chaad Thomas handles all of the details. Chaad also hosts weekly Wine Tastings and annual Wine Education courses. As we said, we take "authentic Italian" to heart.

We like to think of this as a way of thinking about a restaurant as a place for nourishment of both body and of the soul.

For the Procedure

- 4 small lamb loin or lamb filets, 5-6 oz each
- salt and pepper
- 1½ cups Goat Cheese Stuffing (see recipe below)
- kitchen twine
- ½ cup Fig Chutney (see recipe below)
- 2 heads Belgian endive
- 1 bunch (1 lb) asparagus, cleaned and trimmed
- ½ cup Lemon Citronette (see page176)
- all-purpose flour, for dredging
- ½ cup olive oil

For the Goat Cheese Stuffing

- 1½ cups goat cheese
- 2 tbsp mint, minced
- ½ tsp salt
- ½ tsp black pepper
- 1 tbsp milk or cream

For the Fig Chutney

- 1 onion, very small, peeled and diced
- 1 tbsp extra virgin olive oil
- 1 lb figs, black mission (or green figs)
- 1 small orange
- 1 tbsp fresh mint, chopped
- ¼ tsp salt
- pinch of pepper

CARNE — SERVES 4

Carne di Agnello Farcita

GOAT CHEESE STUFFED LAMB LOIN WITH FIG CHUTNEY

I was never a huge fan of fresh figs but I do like dried figs and I really like fig chutney! Many people are familiar with black figs, but where I grew up in Trissino, they were green.

Use dried figs if fresh are not available. When doing so, add juice from one additional orange to the recipe.

FOR THE PROCEDURE

1 Preheat oven at 450°F.

2 Clean, butterfly and pound the meat. The butcher can do this step for you.

3 Lay meat on table, season lightly with salt and pepper.

4 Using a pastry bag without the tip, divide the Goat Cheese Stuffing into the 4 pieces of meat. Roll them up keeping them as tight as possible. Secure with kitchen twine.

5 Heat oil in pan. Dredge the lamb in flour, handling carefully. Sear the meat on all sides until nicely colored.

6 Move lamb onto baking sheet and finish cooking until desired doneness.

7 While it is baking, prepare the salad.

8 Cut Belgian endive in half and core. Cut it into thin strips and place in bowl. Cut the asparagus on the bias, very thinly. Add to the endive. Toss with Lemon Citronette.

FOR THE GOAT CHEESE STUFFING

9 Combine all the ingredients using a wooden spoon. Set aside until meat is prepared.

FOR THE FIG CHUTNEY

10 Sauté onion in olive oil until golden brown. Let cool.

11 Cut the figs into small dice, ⅛-inch pieces.

12 In a bowl zest and juice the entire orange, removing any seeds. Add the figs, onion, chopped mint, salt and pepper. Mix well.

13 Store in an airtight container in the refrigerator. Excess can be frozen if desired.

FOR THE PRESENTATION

14 When lamb is ready, remove from oven and allow to rest a couple minutes before cutting. Remove twine, then slice each piece into thirds on the bias.

15 Place Belgian endive salad on plate and arrange meat on top. Finish the dish by adding about ¼ cup Fig Chutney over meat.

WINE PAIRING '03 OGNISSOLE PRIMITIVO DI MANDURIA

4 8 oz beef tenderloin
2 tbsp fresh rosemary, finely chopped
1 tbsp extra virgin olive oil
2 lemons
salt and pepper
4 tbsp fresh parsley, finely chopped

CARNE — SERVES 4

Filetto di Manzo al Rosmarino

ROSEMARY SCENTED FILET MIGNON

1 Coat filets with the rosemary and oil and let sit overnight.

2 Prepare and heat the grill. When it's ready, start grilling the steaks to desired doneness. When almost ready to remove from grill, squeeze almost half a lemon on each steak. Season with salt and pepper.

FOR THE PRESENTATION

3 Put on serving platter, sprinkle with parsley and more lemon juice.

WINE PAIRING '01 FELSINA CABERNET SAUVIGNON "MAESTRO RARO"

1 cup Grilled Vegetables, chopped (see page 67)
1 cup couscous, cooked
salt and pepper
4 5-6 oz chicken breasts
all-purpose flour, for dredging
½ cup olive oil
4 tbsp butter
2 lemons, zested, seeded and juiced
5-6 oz mixed greens

CARNE — SERVES 4

Pollo Farcito

SUMMER ROASTED STUFFED CHICKEN BREAST WITH COUSCOUS & VEGETABLES

1 Preheat oven to 450°F.

2 Prepare the Grilled Vegetables according to recipe.

3 Prepare the couscous according to the directions on box.

4 Combine vegetables and couscous, seasoning with salt and pepper if needed. Set aside.

5 Cut a pocket deep on side of each chicken breast, and put stuffing into it.

6 Flour chicken on both sides and sear in hot oil. Finish roasting it in the oven, about 20 minutes.

7 In a small pot, melt butter. Add the zest and lemon juice, a pinch of salt and pepper. Boil together.

FOR THE PRESENTATION

8 Serve chicken with a little side of greens and sprinkle with salt and pepper. Drizzle sauce over all.

WINE PAIRING '03 BADIA A COLTIBUONO CHIANTI CLASSICO 'RS

CARNE — SERVES 4

Rotolo di Vitello

STUFFED ROASTED ROLL OF VEAL

This might need a little time to prepare, but it's really worth it! Feel free to use beef tenderloin instead of veal tenderloin if it's easier to find. It will still taste great.

For the Procedure

4 6 oz pieces veal tenderloin
1½ cups Spinach and Ricotta Filling (see recipe below)
½ cup olive oil
all-purpose flour, for dredging meat
salt and pepper
kitchen twine

For the Sauce

4 tbsp butter
8 oz bacon slices, cut into strips
2 shallots, julienned
4 tbsp freshly grated horseradish

For the Spinach and Ricotta Filling, Serves 4–6

1 lbs fresh spinach
2 tbsp olive oil
2 tbsp onion, small dice
1 tsp salt
1 tsp pepper
pinch of nutmeg
¼ cup Parmigiano Reggiano cheese, grated
1 egg
½ cup ricotta cheese

FOR THE PROCEDURE

1 Preheat oven to 500°F.

2 Butterfly and pound the meat about ¼-inch thick. The butcher can prepare it this way for you.

3 Spread the filling on the meat and roll it up. Secure it using kitchen twine in the middle.

4 Heat oil in the pan. Flour meat, then sear it all over until golden in color. Season with salt and pepper. Cover each piece with aluminum foil. Put it on the baking sheet and let cook for 12–15 minutes or until internal temperature reaches 132°F. Remove from oven and let rest.

FOR THE SPINACH AND RICOTTA FILLING

5 Blanch spinach (see page 14) in boiling water. Drain and squeeze excess water from spinach.

6 Cook onions in the oil until translucent. Add spinach and sauté a few minutes, then season with salt, pepper and nutmeg.

7 Set aside and let cool. Grind spinach in food processor, very fine. Add the rest of ingredients mixing well. Store in container and refrigerate until ready to use.

FOR THE SAUCE

8 Melt the butter until it starts to sizzle, add bacon and cook slowly until it gets a little crispy. Add shallots and keep cooking for a couple more minutes. Add horseradish. Set aside.

FOR THE PRESENTATION

9 Remove veal from foil, cut twine off with a sharp knife and cut the rolls in half. Place 2 pieces on top of plated mashed potatoes. Drizzle with a couple tablespoons of sauce.

WINE PAIRING '01 MARCHESE DI PANCRAZI PINOT NERO "VILLA BAGNOLO"

For the Procedure

28 oz swordfish, cut into 1 oz cubes
4 long-rosemary skewers (or 10" wooden skewers)
1 large red onion, cut into 16 pieces
olive oil, for drizzling
24 spears asparagus, more if they are very thin, bottoms removed
1 cup Romesco Sauce (see recipe below)

For the Romesco Sauce

1 tbsp garlic, minced
2 tbsp extra virgin olive oil
1 can diced tomatoes
¾ cup almonds, toasted
¾ cup canned sweet red peppers
salt and pepper

PESCE — SERVES 4

Pesce Spada alla Griglia

SKEWERED GRILLED SWORDFISH WITH SAVORY ALMOND ROMESCO SAUCE

Like Americans, Italians like to grill during the summer. They are not afraid of throwing a whole fish on the grill, head, tail and bones — no big deal! They season it with herbs, salt and pepper and olive oil. That's it — semplice!

FOR THE PROCEDURE

1 Alternate pieces of fish and onion on each skewer, 7 fish, 4 onions on each. Drizzle with a little olive oil.

2 Heat grill. Prepare asparagus by drizzling with olive oil and seasoning with salt and pepper.

3 Start grilling the swordfish, being careful not to overcook it. When you are at the halfway point, begin grilling the asparagus.

FOR THE ROMESCO SAUCE

4 Cook garlic in the oil for a couple minutes. Add the tomatoes and simmer for 20 minutes. Add almonds and peppers and let cook for 5 more minutes.

5 Remove from stove and using immersion blender or the pulse button on the food processor, coarsely chop the sauce. Season with salt and pepper. Store in a small container.

FOR THE PRESENTATION

6 Place asparagus in center of plate, laying the swordfish skewer diagonally across. Top with the Romesco Sauce.

WINE PAIRING '00 CONTRATTO BARBERA D'ASTI "PANTA REI"

½	cup sugar
1	cup water
2	cups prepared espresso coffee
1	cup heavy whipping cream

DOLCE — SERVES 6

Granita al Caffe con Panna

FROZEN ESPRESSO SLUSH

Espresso is to Italians what soda pop is to Americans – is that fair to say? I'd drink, like, 2-3 Espressos a day. Every time I saw a friend on the street I would say, "Let's go have a coffee!" At home, all Italians have "the mocca", a coffee maker, to make coffee. It is not as strong as Espresso, but still pretty strong. I have 6 mocca in my house. Different sizes for different "shot" amounts, 'cause you never know how many people will show up at your door to visit!

1 Combine the sugar and water in a small saucepan and bring it to a boil. Reduce the heat to simmer and cook for about 15 minutes. Add the espresso and stir. Pour the mix into a shallow baking pan and freeze.

2 Check on the freezing mix every 30–40 minutes to scrape the frozen part off. Keep doing that until the whole mixture is a frozen slush consistency.

3 Whip heavy whipping cream until stiff peaks form.

FOR THE PRESENTATION

4 Scoop the frozen espresso slush into glasses and serve topped with the whipped cream.

1½	cups sugar
8	tbsp butter
1	egg
8	oz mascarpone cheese
1	tsp pure vanilla extract
2¼	cups all-purpose flour
½	tsp baking powder
½	cup raisins
½	cup chocolate chips

DOLCE — YIELDS 50 COOKIES

Biscotti al Mascarpone

MASCARPONE BISCUITS

Pastry in Italy is simple. You just don't see the 5 foot tall cakes there like you do in America. Italians eat a lot of what I call dry cookies, made with flour, eggs, sugar, and milk. Often Italians have them for breakfast, as a daytime snack with hot tea or hot milk, or even with a sweet wine for dipping.

1 Preheat oven to 350°F.

2 In a food processor, combine sugar and butter. Add the egg, mascarpone cheese and the vanilla. Mix just until combined. Do not over process.

3 Add the flour and baking powder and process a few seconds to combine. Turn the dough out into a bowl and stir in the chocolate chips and raisins.

4 Using a tablespoon, scoop the dough and drop rounded spoonfuls about 2 inches apart onto a non-stick cookie sheet. Bake until the edges of the cookies are golden, about 25 minutes. Do not brown them. Allow to cool before separating.

WINE PAIRING '98 VILLA LA SELVA VIN SANTO "VIGNA DEL PAPA"

For the Procedure

- 1¼ cups plus 1 tbsp whole milk
- 1 vanilla bean
- 2 tbsp golden raisins
- 1½ tbsp Bacardi rum
- 2 tbsp pine nuts
- 1 tbsp blanched almond slivers
- 5 oz ricotta cheese
- 1½ tbsp sugar
- 2 tsp powdered sugar
- 2 eggs
- 1 egg yolk

For the Caramel

- ½ cup sugar
- 2 tsp lemon juice

DOLCE — YIELDS 5-6 SERVINGS, USING 4 OZ RAMEKINS

Budino di Ricotta

RICOTTA CUSTARD CAKE

A teaspoon of vanilla extract may be used if a vanilla bean is not available; however, using a vanilla bean makes it better.

A Budino is a pudding!

FOR THE PROCEDURE

1 Bring the milk with the vanilla bean to a boil. Remove from heat and split vanilla bean to remove seeds. Scrape them into the milk and throw away the pod.

2 Soak the raisins in the rum until they are plumped.

3 Grind the pine nuts and almonds with the soaked raisins.

4 Combine the milk from the stove with the cheese, sugars and the eggs.

FOR THE CARAMEL

5 Make the caramel by combining sugar and lemon juice in a pot. Stir occasionally with a wooden spoon until it reaches a boil and turns a caramel color. Be careful, it is very hot!

6 Fill the ramekins ⅓ full with the caramel, top with the custard. Place the custard dishes in a larger pan and fill pan with water, halfway up the sides of the ramekins. Bake for 1 hour at 400°F. Let cool before serving.

WINE PAIRING '98 BERBERANI MOSCATO PASSITO "MONTICELLO"

DOLCE — SERVES 8-10

Torta di Prugne

RUSTIC PLUM TART

For the Crust

1½ cups all-purpose flour
2 tbsp granulated sugar
½ tsp salt
½ cup unsalted butter, chilled, cut into ½-inch pieces
ice water

For the Topping

1½ lbs plums, halved, pitted and cut into 6 pieces
6 tbsp granulated sugar
2 tbsp fresh ginger, grated
½ tsp ground cinnamon
1 tbsp all-purpose flour
2 tbsp unsalted butter, melted
1 egg, beaten
¼ cup apricot preserves

FOR THE CRUST

1 Blend the flour, sugar and the salt in a food processor. Add the butter, using the on/off pulse, until the mixture resembles a coarse meal.

2 Add 2 tbsp of ice water; blend until moist clumps form, adding more water by teaspoonfuls if mixture is dry.

3 Gather the dough into a ball, flatten into a disk and wrap in plastic. Refrigerate for at least one hour.

FOR THE TOPPING

4 Preheat oven to 400°F.

5 Toss the plums, 4 tbsp of sugar, ginger, and cinnamon in a bowl.

6 Roll out the dough on a baking sheet. Place into a 9-inch tart pan, preferably with removable bottom. Press dough down along inside edges of pan and up the sides. Remove any extra dough. Mix 1 tbsp of sugar and 1 tbsp of flour in a small bowl. Sprinkle it over the dough, leaving a 2-inch plain border.

7 Arrange the plums in concentric circles on the dough, leaving the border empty. Drizzle with melted butter. Fold the dough border towards the center. Brush the border with the egg glaze (beaten egg), sprinkle with 1 tbsp sugar.

8 Bake the tart until the plums are tender and the crust is golden, about 45 minutes.

9 Stir the preserves in a sauce pan over low heat until melted. Brush preserves over the plums. Cool the tart for 1 hour on a baking sheet.

10 Allow to cool slightly. Remove from pan and transfer the tart onto a serving platter. Serve at room temperature.

WINE PAIRING '03 BRUNO VERDI "SANGUE DI GIUDA"

The fall is just a whole new chapter of cooking ideas. Between the smell and the colors of the new vegetables and fruit—oh boy! My head starts spinning, searching for the best food I can prepare!

As a little girl I used to go hunting for mushrooms with my papá and sorella, Graziella. But, in addition to our adventures into the woods, we would go to my nonno's to pick the grapes. He owns a small part of a vineyard right next to the house and we would trot along beside him to the grape barrels that held the day's pickings. He would lift the two of us into these huge barrels of grapes and we would stomp on them, squishing the grapes between our toes, "a piedi-nudi" [bare foot]. It was great fun! It isn't surprising that I had my first tastes of wine when I was little.

autunno

AUTUMN

1 10–12 oz pork tenderloin
1 tbsp fresh sage, chopped
1 tbsp fresh rosemary, chopped
2 tbsp garlic, minced
olive oil
1 lb mixed mushrooms
1 tbsp butter
1 tsp garlic, chopped
salt and pepper

2 cups variety of squash, diced
1 tbsp olive oil
3 cups black cabbage, sliced (if unavailable, use kale)
olive oil
12 small slices of sourdough or focaccia bread, about 3 x 4 inches
1–2 garlic cloves, peeled to rub bread after toasted

ANTIPASTO — SERVES 4

Trio di Bruschetta

ISABELLA'S AUTUMN ITALIAN TOASTS

As we did with the summer menu, we are serving this assorted toasted garlic bread with seasonal ingredients. One slice will be topped with a variety of squashes, one with seasonal mushrooms, and one with black cabbage and roasted pork. Use a mixture of butternut, acorn and pumpkin squashes. Remember, any leftover squash can be used for pasta or soup dishes. Try and find some chanterelle, black trumpet or porcini mushrooms. They make such a wonderful combination and will give you a real earthy taste. Otherwise, use shitake, oyster and portobello, which should be easy to find in your local market.

1 Season the pork with the fresh chopped sage, rosemary and garlic. Rub with a little olive oil and roast the meat at 350°F for 20-30 minutes or until internal temperature reaches 145°F with a meat thermometer. Let it cool. Slice the meat very thin and keep it on the side.

2 Slice the mushrooms as thin as possible. Sauté in a tablespoon of butter and a teaspoon of chopped garlic. Season with salt and pepper and set aside.

3 Sauté squashes in a tablespoon of olive oil. Season with salt and pepper. Cook until tender, and then set aside.

All this could be done ahead of time, then just before serving, reheat in the oven. It would make it much easier than handling three different pans at the same time!

4 Sauté the cabbage with a little olive oil. This is best done at the time of serving.

5 Add the sliced pork to it and toss it to make sure it is hot.

6 While you are doing all this, toast the bread in the oven, and then rub it with the garlic clove.

FOR THE PRESENTATION

7 Divide each of the toppings onto 4 slices of bread. Put one of each bruschetta onto 4 different plates. Drizzle each with a little extra virgin olive oil, and then serve.

WINE PAIRING '04 MARCHESE DI BAROLO DOLCETTO D'ALBA "MADONNA DI COMO"

½ bottle chardonnay
1 garlic clove
2 bay leaves
20 large shrimp, peeled and de-veined
4 oz butter, softened
mushroom powder, as described below

ANTIPASTO — SERVES 4

Gamberi in Crosta di Funghi con Burro al Chardonnay

ROASTED MUSHROOM CRUSTED SHRIMP WITH CHARDONNAY BUTTER

There are lots of mushrooms in the Veneto region. I remember going with my sorella and my papá walking in the woods going on mushroom hunts. Sometimes we would go for 3 hours and find nothing and say okay and then go home, but most of the time we would find all sorts of mushrooms, black trumpets and chanterelles. The searching might be hard, but the hardest part is the cleaning. That we left to my mamma.

Enjoy that other half bottle of chardonnay while you are preparing the dish...you know—half for the recipe— half for you! I like good wine too.

1 In a small pot, pour the wine with the garlic and bay leaves. Bring it to a boil until you are left with ½ cup of wine reduction.

2 Preheat the oven to 475°F.

3 Take the shrimp and cut them in the middle and open (butterfly). Then, coat both sides with the mushroom powder. Lay on a baking sheet. Season lightly with salt and pepper. Put them in oven until done, about 10 minutes. Display shrimp on serving platter and finish the sauce.

4 Bring the chardonnay again to a boil. Little by little add the butter to make it whip, not melt, using a whisk and shaking the pan back and forth.

FOR THE PRESENTATION

5 Pour the sauce over the shrimp, garnish with some greens and serve.

You will need a mixture of dried mushrooms for this appetizer. You should be able to find little packets of dried porcini, morels and shitake mushrooms at your local specialty store or in the fresh vegetable section of your grocery store. Combine the mushrooms and grind them in a food processor until you get a fine consistency.

WINE PAIRING '01 INAMA SOAVE CLASSICO "VIGNETO DU LOT'

1 cup black seedless grapes, de-stemmed, cut in half if very large
1 tsp fennel seeds
2 tsp sugar
1 tsp cinnamon
1 tbsp orange zest
2 tbsp fresh orange juice

1 butternut squash, with long "neck," cut into strings
2 tbsp olive oil
salt and pepper
4 tbsp butter, in 2 oz pads
½ cup red wine
½ cup fresh ricotta
2 tbsp chopped pistachios

ANTIPASTO — SERVES 4

"Pasta" di Zucca in Tempo di Vendemmia

PUMPKIN SPAGHETTI PASTA OF HARVEST TIME

A "turning slicer" will make this dish a lot easier to prepare. You can purchase one at www.famousfood.com. There is another gadget called a julienne peeler that looks like a potato peeler with teeth. It is readily available and cheaper. It won't give you spaghetti-like strands but you will get thin pieces. It might be worthwhile to purchase one of these kitchen tools; otherwise you'll need to cut the squash by hand. Might be a big pain in the butt! Use the top part of the butternut squash. It has no seeds and its shape makes it easy to form the "spaghetti". Have four pasta bowls ready on the side of the stove. This is a very quick and easy dish to make. It is very colorful, very nice, and very good.

1 Season the grapes with fennel seeds, cinnamon, sugar and orange. Toss very well and set aside.

2 Peel the squash and then slice it very, very thin. Then slice each slice into thin strings, to resemble spaghetti unless you have already made the "strings" with the spiral slicer. Set this aside.

3 Heat the olive oil in a large pan. Add squash strings, season lightly with salt and pepper and toss for 2–3 minutes. Do not overcook the squash as it will fall apart.

4 Almost at the same time, get the grapes going. Heat ½ of the butter in a different pan. When it starts to sizzle, add the grapes and let cook for a couple of minutes. The grapes will start to wilt a little and at this point, add the red wine and bring the sauce to a boil.

FOR THE PRESENTATION

5 Remove grapes from sauce and put back on stove, bring to a boil again and add the rest of the butter, shaking the pan back and forth until it's all melted. If, after adding the butter to the sauce it starts to "break" and separate, add 1 teaspoon of water and shake it until it looks smooth and "all together."

6 Divide some of the sauce on the bottom of 4 bowls or plates (it looks great on a white plate). Place bundles of squash on top, reserved grapes and remaining sauce. Garnish with ricotta and pistachios.

WINE PAIRING '04 SCARBOLO TOCAI FRIULANO

For the Stew

- 1 cup dried beans, soaked overnight, then drained
- 2 tbsp extra virgin olive oil
- 1 tsp chopped garlic
- ¼ cup tomato sauce
- 5-6 sage leaves
- salt and pepper
- 4 slices sourdough bread
- 1 cup Duck Sausage Sauce (see recipe below), reheated

For the Duck Sausage Sauce

- 2 tbsp olive oil
- 1 tsp garlic, chopped
- 2 tbsp onion, minced
- 2 tbsp carrot, minced
- 2 tbsp celery stalk, minced
- 1 tbsp fresh sage, chopped
- 1 tbsp fresh rosemary, chopped
- salt and pepper
- 4 oz pancetta
- 1 lbs ground duck meat
- ½ cup white wine

ANTIPASTO — SERVES 4

Fagioli Borlotti in Umido, con Crostone di Salsiccia d'Anatra

BORLOTTI BEAN STEW AND DUCK SAUSAGE CROSTONE

Beans too, are one of my favorite foods. This bean stew is just like my mamma would make, very simple. In Italy, simple is good—che buona! My papá's way to enjoy beans is to boil them and add thinly sliced onions, salt, pepper, olive oil and a touch of vinegar. My papá likes to make Pasta e Fagioli too. To it, he would add cotica [pork skin]. He would cook it all together until it gets very soft. He really likes that!

Barlotti beans are a kind of Italian bean. It's okay to use kidney beans or cranberry beans if barlotti are not available.

This is a big batch of sauce! Of course you can use it as pasta sauce or you could always freeze it in small portions for future use.

FOR THE STEW

1 Boil the beans starting with fresh, cold water. Cook until tender, about 1 hour. Drain beans, reserving some of the water in case you need to adjust the stew.

2 Heat oil in a pan, add garlic and when it starts to sizzle add the beans. Add about 2 oz of the cooking water and tomato sauce. Let boil for a couple of minutes. Add sage and season with salt and pepper.

3 While beans are simmering, toast or grill the bread. If you wish, rub lightly with a garlic clove.

FOR THE DUCK SAUSAGE SAUCE

4 Heat the oil in a pot. Add the garlic and vegetables and slightly brown them. Add the herbs and let cook for a couple of minutes.

5 Meanwhile, chop up the pancetta , then add to food processor to grind it even further. Add the pancetta to the pan and let cook for another 2-3 minutes.

6 Put the duck meat in and stir well. Allow it to cook until the duck meat is very well done, then add white wine. After the alcohol has evaporated, add 1½ cups of water to the pot. Let this simmer for 20 minutes or so. Taste for salt and pepper.

FOR THE PRESENTATION

7 Put bean stew in a bowl and place crostone on top. Then ladle Duck Sausage Sauce over all. Garnish with sage leaves.

WINE PAIRING '03 MASI "MODELLO DELLE VENEZIE"

2	small apples, Granny Smith
2	tbsp olive oil
½	cup raisins
4	2 oz slices of smoked ricotta
	chestnut honey

ANTIPASTO O DOLCE — SERVES 4

Ricotta Affumicata con Miele di Castagno

SMOKED RICOTTA WITH CHESTNUT HONEY

This is a very tasty and simple dish that could easily be served as dessert as well as an appetizer. Remember, simplice e buona! It is so typical for Italians to eat fruit and cheese together, as common as Americans to eat peanut butter and jelly. If your grocer does not carry the smoked ricotta, check out the local specialty stores or see if it can be ordered for you. Otherwise, use regular ricotta, ricotta salata, baked smoked ricotta, or baked unsmoked ricotta cheese—or even the French aged goat's cheese, Boucheron. Be creative, have fun!

1 Quarter, peel and core apples. Cut each section into 3 pieces. Heat the oil in a pan and add apples. Cook until they start to color.

2 Add raisins and let cook for a couple minutes.

FOR THE PRESENTATION

3 Divide the cheese on a platter or 4 small plates. Divide the fruit a little on top of the cheese, a little on the side. Drizzle over with the chestnut honey. Enjoy!

WINE PAIRING PIEROPAN '01 RECIOTO DI SOAVE "LE COLOMBARE"

Sará buono saltato in padella o fritto?

For the Pizza

½ cup butternut squash
1 Pizza Dough Crust (see page 166)
1 tbsp olive oil
½ cup onion, sliced
salt and pepper
½ cup farm cheese (or Lemon Ricotta, see page 108)
2 tbsp Sage Oil (see recipe below)

For the Sage Oil

½ cup fresh sage, finely chopped
1½ cups olive oil

ANTIPASTO — SERVES 4

Pizza con Zucca D'autunno

PIZZA WITH FALL BUTTERNUT SQUASH

Sometimes it's hard to find fresh farm cheese—so okay—you can use soft farmer's cheese. Just, don't use the yellow one that looks like packaged mozzarella!

FOR THE PIZZA

1 Peel and cut squash into small cubes. Season with salt, pepper and olive oil. Bake in 450°F oven for 25–30 minutes.

2 Heat olive oil in a pan. Add onion and let cook until it gets a caramelized color and taste. Stir onion once in a while to make sure you obtain a uniform result. Season with salt and pepper.

3 Preheat oven to 500°F.

4 Brush a little sage oil on the crust. Spread onions and butternut squash all over. Divide the cheese on top. Bake until the crust is well done, about 15–20 minutes.

5 Before serving the pizza, drizzle more sage oil over it.

FOR THE SAGE OIL

6 Mix the ingredients together in a tall container or cup.

7 Using a hand mixer, grind or purée the mixture. If you don't have a hand mixer use a food processor, making sure to add the oil a little at a time with the processor running.

WINE PAIRING '02 MASI VALPOLICELLA CLASSICO

For the Filet

- 2 8 oz beef filets
- 2 tbsp fresh rosemary, chopped
- 1–2 lbs coarse sea salt
- ½ cup cold water

For the Insalatina

- 2 cups of cooked squash (see page 98)
- ½ cup raisins
- 3 cups red oak lettuce
- 3 tbsp balsamic vinegar
- 2 tbsp extra virgin olive oil
- salt and pepper, for seasoning

CARNE O ANTIPASTO — SERVES 2 OR 4 AS APPETIZER

Filetto di Manzo in Crosta di Sale con Insalatina Autunnale

FILET OF BEEF IN A SALT CRUST WITH FALL SALAD

This is another version of my making Americans happy so they can eat their salads as a meal. As I explained in the summer chapter, in Italy there is no fuss made with salads, most of the time they are just mixed greens! I have enjoyed creating new recipes that make Paesano's customers so happy.

For only a few people you could use the 8 oz filet. If you are thinking of doing this for more than 10-12 people use a whole beef tenderloin. After baking the meat with salt encrusted around it, you are in for a juicy treat with much flavor!

FOR THE FILET

1 Preheat the oven to 450°F.

2 Rub the meat with the chopped rosemary.

3 Put the salt in a bowl, add water and toss all together to make it a little pliable.

4 Get a pan big enough to hold the meat. Line it with a large piece of aluminum foil. Put a layer of salt on the foil, about ¼-inch thick. Lay the meat on top. Add another layer of salt, about ¼-inch thick on top of the meat. Press it with your hand to make sure the meat is covered all around. Wrap the foil up around the meat covering all sides. Repeat with the second piece of meat.

5 Place the pan in the oven and bake until it reaches an inside temperature of 120–125°F (for rare) or 130–135°F (for medium rare). When it is done, remove the meat to a separate pan and let cool still wrapped in foil.

FOR THE INSALATINA

6 Sauté the squash in the pan and add raisins long enough to plump them.

7 Clean lettuce and break leaves with your hands. Put in a bowl with the squash and raisins. Season with vinegar and olive oil and salt and pepper. Set aside.

FOR THE PRESENTATION

8 Take the meat and scrape salt off. Wipe excess salt with a damp cloth or quickly rinse it under running water – pat dry.

9 Slice meat about ⅛-inch thick. Take large lettuces leaves and place on a plate. Arrange sliced meat around the outside and place fall salad in the middle. Drizzle a little extra virgin olive oil on the meat and cracked black pepper and serve.

WINE PAIRING '03 ANIME VALPOLICELLA

For the Zucchini

½ tbsp garlic, chopped
¼ cup fresh parsley, chopped
½ cup olive oil
pinch of salt and pepper
2 zucchini

For the Lemon Ricotta Mix

1½ cups fresh ricotta
1 tsp salt
½ tsp black pepper
1 lemon, zest and juice

ANTIPASTO — SERVES 4

Rollotini di Zucchini con Ricotta al Limone

GRILLED ZUCCHINI ROLLS WITH LEMON RICOTTA

FOR THE ZUCCHINI

1 Make the garlic parsley oil by mixing the first 5 ingredients together.

2 Slice the zucchini to ⅛-inch thick, lengthwise.

3 Grill the zucchini and lay them on a sheet pan. Brush each slice with the seasoned oil and allow to cool.

FOR THE LEMON RICOTTA MIX

4 Combine all ingredients and set aside.

FOR THE PRESENTATION

5 Lay 2 slices of the zucchini next to each other so they overlap slightly. Put about 1 tbsp of the Lemon Ricotta mixture on them and then roll them up. Continue rolling until all of the zucchini and filling are used. Store the rolls on a small sheet pan until ready to serve. Serve with grilled or toasted bread.

WINE PAIRING '04 MACULAN "PINO & TOI"

- 2 cups black seedless grapes, de-stemmed
- 3 cups butternut squash, cut in small dice, about ½-inch
- 2 apples, peeled and cored, cut into 12 wedges each
- 2 tbsp olive oil
- ½ cup aged ricotta cheese, shaved (or your choice of cheese)
- 2 heads red oak lettuce, washed, patted dry
- ½ cup Black Grape Dressing (see page 177)

INSALATA — SERVES 4

Insalata Dai Colori Autunnali

COLORS OF THE SEASON SALAD

1 Preheat oven to 450°F.

2 Combine grapes, apples and squash on a baking sheet with the oil. Roast for about 20–25 minutes or until the grapes start to cook and the apples get some nice color.

3 Put them in a bowl. Tear the lettuce for the salad, reserving some whole leaves for garnish. Add dressing and toss very well.

FOR THE PRESENTATION

4 Place reserved large leaves on 4 plates as "bed" for salad. Place tossed salad on top and sprinkle with ricotta cheese.

WINE PAIRING '04 ALLEGRINI SOAVE

INSALATA — SERVES 4

Insalata di Fine Estate

INDIAN SUMMER SALAD

Probably the meat I ate most as a child was pork. Sometimes it was the centerpiece of a dish and sometimes it would just be for the flavoring. In this salad, I use the bacon strips. If you can find apple wood smoked bacon, it would be great! Smoked and cured meats are eaten all over the Veneto region so there is a little bit of home tucked into this summer salad.

Gnudi are actually dumplings from Southern Italy, but they sounded so good I added them to the salad.

For the Salad

- 8 nice large leaves of red Bibb lettuce
- 1 small head red Bibb lettuce
- 12 oz bacon strips, cut into small pieces
- 1 lb assorted mushrooms, thinly sliced
- salt and pepper
- 12 "Gnudi" Dumplings, for garnish (see recipe below)
- ¾ cup Cider Vinaigrette (see page 177)

For the Gnudi Dumplings

- 1 cup ricotta cheese
- 2 eggs
- ½ cup bread flour
- ¼ cup Parmigiano Reggiano cheese, grated
- 1 tbsp fresh sage, chopped
- ½ tsp salt
- pinch of nutmeg
- 1 cup semolina, to coat dumplings
- oil for frying

FOR THE SALAD

1 Gently wash the large outer leaves of Bibb lettuce and keep them on the side. They will be used to garnish the plates.

2 Cut the head of lettuce into smaller pieces after washing it. Place in salad bowl.

3 Heat a pan and sauté the bacon enough for it to release some of the fat. Add mushrooms and let cook for a couple more minutes. Season with salt and pepper. Add to the bowl.

4 Add the Cider Vinaigrette and stir well.

FOR THE GNUDI DUMPLINGS

5 Combine the first 7 ingredients in a large bowl. Make sure to mix it all very well. Cover and refrigerate until it's ready to be used. The mixture will be sticky.

6 Form dumplings to about the size of a walnut or slightly smaller. Wet your hands with cold water. Lay them in the semolina as soon as they are formed, coating them very well. Place them on a sprayed sheet tray until you are ready to fry them all. They need to be nicely golden brown in color to make sure the flour is cooked all the way through.

FOR THE PRESENTATION

7 Divide salad between 4 large plates. Lay 2 leaves on the side of each salad to make it look kind of like a bowl. Display 3 fried dumplings on each plate. Serve.

WINE PAIRING '04 SCARBOLO TOCAI FRIULANO

For the Filling

- 1 lb black cabbage
- 1 leek
- ½ cup olive oil
- 1 cup quartered, canned artichoke hearts, drained
- 2 cups farm cheese, (use soft farmers cheese if farm cheese not available)
- ½ cup Parmigiano Reggiano cheese, grated
- 1 egg
- 1 tsp salt
- ½ tsp black pepper

For the Sauce

- 1 cup whole milk
- ¼ tsp nutmeg
- ½ tsp salt
- ½ tsp black pepper
- 1 oz roux (1 tbsp butter and 1 tbsp bread flour combined to make a paste)
- ½ cup tomato sauce, homemade or canned
- ½ cup vegetable stock or water

PASTA — SERVES 4

Cannelloni Farciti al Cavolo Nero e Formaggio di Latteria

BLACK CABBAGE AND FARM CHEESE CANNELLONI

Black cabbage is a stronger flavor than both green and purple cabbage, but if you like cabbage you will most likely enjoy this too.

FOR THE FILLING

1 Rinse and julienne the black cabbage. Drain and set aside.

2 Wash and slice the leeks being careful to get any dirt out of the inner layers. Drain and set aside.

3 Heat half of the olive oil in a large sauté pan. Add the black cabbage and sauté until wilted. Set aside to cool.

4 Heat the other half of the olive oil and sauté the leeks until wilted too. Set aside to cool.

5 Using a food processor, grind the artichokes and put them in a bowl. Grind the cooked cabbage and leeks as soon as they are cool enough and add them to the same bowl. Add all of the remaining ingredients and mix well. Store in a container until ready to use.

FOR THE SAUCE

6 Put the milk in a small stockpot. Add the seasoning and bring to a boil.

7 Meanwhile, melt the butter in a small pan and add the flour to make a roux. Cook the "paste" for at least 3 minutes, stirring occasionally to avoid burning.

8 When the milk boils, you can add the roux. Stir well and reduce the heat to a simmer. Cook for about 10–15 minutes, stirring occasionally.

9 Add the tomato sauce and keep simmering for another 5 minutes.

10 Remove from the heat and add ¼ cup of vegetable stock (or water). Smooth out the sauce with the immersion blender. Store in a container until ready to use.

WINE PAIRING '03 CANTINE SANT'AGATA BARBERA D'ASTI "BABY BARB"

For the Procedure

4 large pasta sheets (or 8 small)
¼ cup Parmigiano Reggiano cheese
2 tbsp butter

FOR THE PROCEDURE

11 Preheat oven to 450°F.

12 Heat 2 gallons of water with 2 tablespoons salt.

13 Prepare a separate pan with iced water.

14 Cook the pasta for 2–3 minutes in the boiling water and shock it cool in the ice water.

15 Lay them out on a sheet pan. Take each sheet and trim the edge if necessary. If you are using large sheets, cut them in half to obtain 2 cannelloni sheets. Each sheet should be about 6 x 4 inches.

16 Spoon a little less than ⅓ cup of the filling on each cannel-loni sheet using a pastry bag or simply a spoon. Roll them up length-wise keeping them tight.

17 Lay on a buttered baking pan or sheet tray. Melt the butter, brush it on the cannelloni, sprinkle with cheese and bake for at least 20–25 minutes. They will get a nice golden color on top.

FOR THE PRESENTATION

18 Put about 4 oz of heated sauce on the bottom of the plates, lay 2 cannelloni on each plate, crosswise, garnish with fried leeks (if you wish) then serve.

- 20 oz gnocchi, homemade (Winter Potato Gnocchi, page 150) or high quality frozen product
- 4 tbsp butter
- ½ cup shallots, thinly sliced
- 2 tbsp garlic, minced
- 3 cups assorted mushrooms (Chanterelle, porcini, black trumpet, morels)
- salt and pepper
- ½ cup heavy cream
- 1 tsp fresh rosemary, chopped
- ¼ cup walnuts, toasted and chopped

PASTA — SERVES 4

Gnocchi con Varietá di Funghi Autunnale

GNOCCHI WITH FALL WILD MUSHROOM VARIETY

Fresh mushrooms need to be cleaned very well to remove any dirt. Usually chanterelle, black trumpets and morels do not need to be cut; porcini, on the other hand, should be sliced or small diced. If you are not able to find any of these mushrooms—no problem—just get whatever the market offers, just as you would for the bruschetta.

1 In a large pan melt the butter; add shallots and garlic and let cook for a few minutes. Add mushrooms and keep cooking for another 3–4 minutes. Season with salt and pepper.

2 While you are doing all this, bring a pot of water to boil for the gnocchi. (Remember to add some salt to the water!)

3 Add the cream to the mushrooms and let it reduce a little.

4 Drop gnocchi into the boiling water. They are ready when they float, but remember to let them cook a couple minutes longer.

FOR THE PRESENTATION

5 Using a strainer, take the gnocchi out of the water, and then add them to the pan. Stir carefully to mix everything together. Serve on plates and sprinkle with rosemary and walnuts.

WINE PAIRING '03 CORTE FORTE VALPOLICELLA CLASSICO

20 large shrimp, peeled and deveined
2 cups leeks, sliced thinly
salt and pepper
2 cups butternut squash, cubed (see page 105)
1 lb cavatelli or 20 oz of gnocchi (see page 150)
¼ cup extra virgin olive oil

PASTA — SERVES 4

Cavatelli con la Zucca e Porri

CAVATELLI WITH AUTUMN SQUASH AND LEEKS

Cavatelli is very typical Italian pasta that is featured in this recipe. Just as good, you can try it with potato gnocchi. It's easy, healthy and quick!

1 Bring a large pot of water, seasoned with salt, to a boil.

2 In a large pan pour the oil. Add the shrimp and let cook 2 minutes on each side. Add leeks and some salt and pepper to season. Stir well. Add squash to it until it warms up. If using raw squash, add it at first before adding anything else because it takes longer than shrimp to cook, about 10–12 minutes.

3 You should drop your pasta in the water when you are starting the sauce. It will be ready just about the same time Add drained pasta to the sauce and toss well. Serve.

WINE PAIRING '03 CA' RUGATE SOAVE CLASSICO "SAN MICHELE"

To Marinate the Duck Breasts

4 10–12 oz duck breasts, skin on (if you come across a bigger breast (16–17 oz), it's still okay, just get two!)
¼ cup soy sauce
1 cup balsamic vinegar
½ cup honey
¼ cup maple syrup
1 tsp garlic, minced
1 tbsp pink peppercorn
¼ tsp ground black pepper

For the Poached Pears

2 pears
3 cups Moscato wine
½ cup granulated sugar
1 cinnamon stick
2 whole cloves

For the Pear Chips

1 pear

CARNE – SERVES 4

Petto d'Anatra Marinato alla Griglia

GRILLED MARINATED DUCK BREAST WITH MOSCATO POACHED PEARS AND PEAR CHIPS

Fowl is very common in the Veneto region. Depending on the season, different fowl are more readily available. Hen, pigeon, and duck are frequently used on fall and winter menus; chicken is pretty much eaten year-round. Here, I have complemented the duck with a sweet Moscato wine and poached pears. This is so tasty and makes for a beautiful presentation. We would make this for a very special holiday.

This process might take a while so you could prepare the chips far ahead of time. They will last a few days if kept in an airtight container.

If you don't have a grill, you could sear the duck in a pan, skin side down first, to make it crispy. Then turn to the other side and finish it in the oven, at 450°F for about 10 minutes.

TO MARINATE THE DUCK BREASTS

1 Mix all ingredients together. Don't worry if you cannot find the pink peppercorn, do without it. Marinate the duck breast in marinade at least overnight. It could actually be left for 2–3 days with no problem. Discard the marinade when you are ready to grill.

2 Grill the meat to your own liking. I suggest keeping it to a medium rare temperature.

3 Let it rest for 5–10 minutes before slicing. This would help retain the moisture and flavor and maintain a more even temperature throughout.

FOR THE POACHED PEARS

4 Peel the pears. Put them in a small pot. Cover with the wine, sugar and spices. Put the pot on the stove and bring it to a boil. Reduce the heat to a simmer. Simmer just until tender. Do not over do! Let cool.

5 Remove the pears from the cooking liquid. It will be used as the sauce for the duck breast. Cut the pears in half and fan them. Keep on the side until ready to serve.

6 Put the cooking liquid back on the stove and let reduce to a more syrupy consistency.

FOR THE PEAR CHIPS

7 Preheat oven to 200°F. Place lightly-sprayed parchment paper on baking sheet.

8 Wash pears. Do not remove peel. Cut off the bottom of the pears and slice about ⅛-inch thick on a slicer or a mandoline. Lay the pear slices on the sheet tray without them touching each other. Bake for 1 hour. They will begin to color and start drying out. Let cool before storing in a container.

FOR THE PRESENTATION

9 When the meat is ready, display fanned pear on plate. Next to it, place the duck, also fanned, and drizzle the moscato syrup over all. Garnish with 2–3 slices of pear chips and serve with some butternut squash if you wish.

WINE PAIRING '00 ALLEGRINI AMARONE DELLA VALPOLICELLA CLASSICO

For the Marinade

1 guinea fowl (hen)
1 small onion
1 stalk of celery
1 carrot
1 sprig fresh rosemary
2 fresh sprigs sage
4 garlic cloves, peeled
3 cups white wine

For the Procedure

1 cup olive oil
6 oz pancetta, cut into small strips
1 fennel, cut in half and sliced
1 medium red onion, thinly sliced
1 tsp fresh rosemary, chopped
salt and pepper
1–2 cups vegetable stock or chicken stock

CARNE — SERVES 4

Faraona Arrosto con il Finocchio

ROASTED GUINEA FOWL WITH FENNEL

First of all, we don't eat much turkey like in America so my mamma used to cook lots of Faraona [guinea fowl] which personally, I find more tasty than turkey.

FOR THE MARINADE

1 Take the bird and trim off the wing tips. Trim off any excess skin and fat around the neck and hind end. Split the bird and cut each half into 4 pieces. Put all the pieces into a large container.

2 Coarsely chop the vegetables and combine them with the herbs and wine. Pour this marinade over the fowl pieces. Cover with a lid for 2–3 days and refrigerate.

FOR THE PROCEDURE

3 Heat the oil in a large pan. Drain the fowl from the marinade and pat dry. Put the meat, skin side down and let sear for 2–3 minutes. Turn to the other side for another 2–3 minutes.

4 Add the pancetta, fennel, onion and rosemary. Shake the pan back and forth to make sure ingredients are well spread out.

5 If the pan looks too crowded, just move the fowl to a larger baking pan. Season with salt and pepper, add 1 cup vegetable stock and roast it, covered, in a 450°F preheated oven for 40–50 minutes.

6 Take a look once in a while, in case you need to add some more stock, so it won't dry out. Adjust with seasoning if necessary. Remember, the pancetta is pretty salty so go light with the seasoning.

FOR THE PRESENTATION

7 Serve the fowl on top of mashed potatoes, dividing equally onto 4 serving plates. Arrange pieces of fennel, onions and pancetta on plate and ladle juice over all.

WINE PAIRING '02 ASTIBARBERA BARBERA D'ASTI "CLAUDIUS"

For the Chianti Reduction

1 bottle Chianti wine
2 tbsp shallots, small diced
2 bay leaves
2 tbsp beef base

For the Fig Crust

½ lb fresh figs, use dried ones if not available
½ lb gorgonzola cheese

For the Procedure

½ cup olive oil
4 8 oz pieces of beef tenderloin, center cut
1 recipe fig crust
1 recipe Chianti reduction
4 tbsp butter, cut into small dice

CARNE — SERVES 4

Filetto di Manzo in Crosta di Fichi e Gorgonzola

FIG AND GORGONZOLA CRUSTED FILET MIGNON WITH A CHIANTI REDUCTION

I very often combine figs and Gorgonzola. It is a classic fruit and cheese combination used in appetizers as well as desserts. Here it forms a crust on top of a filet that is then covered with a velvety Chianti sauce.

FOR THE CHIANTI REDUCTION

1 Combine all in a small pan. Bring to a boil. Reduce it by ⅓. Pour through a stainer and reserve reduction.

FOR THE FIG CRUST

2 If using dry figs, cover them in hot water for 20–30 minutes until they get soft. Drain them, and using a food processor, grind figs into very small pieces. Put in a bowl. Grind gorgonzola too, or better yet, grate it using a cheese grater. Mix the two ingredients together.

FOR THE PROCEDURE

3 Preheat oven to 450°F.

4 Heat oil in a pan. Make sure it's very hot before you start searing the meat. Add all 4 pieces of meat to the pan and sear one side for 2–3 minutes. Turn over and sear the other side for 2–3 minutes. Place on an oiled baking sheet or pan.

5 Divide the crust into the 4 filets and press down with your fingers to get the top part all covered. Put in the oven until desired doneness. When the filets are ready, let them rest for a few minutes before serving.

6 While the meat is resting, adjust the sauce. Put the Chianti reduction into a large pan. Bring it back to a boil. Add the pieces of butter, a few at a time, shaking the pan back and forth until it starts to thicken. You shouldn't make the sauce too early, otherwise it will separate. If that happens anyway, just add a little hot water to the wine. It will bring it back to the right consistency.

FOR THE PRESENTATION

7 Serve the filet on top of roasted potatoes, and then drizzle with the Chianti sauce.

WINE PAIRING '02 MACULAN BRENTINO ROSSO

Maiale

The Veneto region, like much of Italy, is known for all of its pork products. Prosciutto is a sweet, delicate, uncooked ham preserved by curing or air-drying, and is served in thin slices as an antipasto. Pancetta is the same cut of pork as bacon, cured with salt, not smoked. It is often rolled up like large salami. Pancetta serves as a subtle, important role for flavoring recipes. Pork dishes are only limited by the imagination of the Italian cook. You can just go crazy! Growing up, I ate pork as much as I ate polenta and cheese.

For the Herb Marinade

1 tbsp fresh rosemary, chopped
1 tbsp fresh sage, chopped
½ cup olive oil

For the Procedure

8–10 Yukon gold potatoes (if medium sized)
2 lbs pork tenderloin
8 10-inch long wood skewers, soaked in water to avoid burning on grill

For the Sauce

2 tbsp butter, for cooking
2 cups Seasoned Grapes (see page 100)
¾ cup red wine
2 tbsp butter, cubes

CARNE — SERVES 4

Spiedini di Filetto di Maiale e Patate

FIRE GRILLED SKEWERS OF SAGE SCENTED PORK TENDERLOIN WITH BLACK GRAPE SAUCE

Most Northern Italian families rely on pork for the meat in their diet. As a child, I would go with my papá to get the pig from the farmer. They would slaughter it there and process the whole thing. A big wooden table sat in the middle of the room and they would crank out the sausages from a machine sitting on top of it. They would grind the meat, do whatever you wanted. No problem! All kinds of sausages, pork salami, everything from the pig would be hanging from the ceiling. We would help [well, maybe I watched], butcher the pig. I would eat the raw ground pork right there. Sometimes they would have the fireplace going and we would cook it and eat it with fresh bread and wine. With the Italians love of pork, grilling and wine this recipe is like comfort food.

FOR THE HERB MARINADE

1 Combine the above ingredients and set aside.

FOR THE PROCEDURE

2 Bring a small pot of water to a boil. Cut small potatoes in half, or larger potatoes into 3-inch wide pieces. Boil the potatoes until they are done, but be careful of not overcooking them. Drain them and let them cool.

3 Clean excess fat from the meat. Cut the tenderloin into 1 oz pieces, at least, maybe a little bigger.

4 When all is ready, skewer potato and meat, alternating them and making sure to have 3 pieces of each on each skewer. Lie on a tray and drizzle with the Herb Marinade until you are ready to grill them.

FOR THE SAUCE

5 Melt 2 tbsp butter in a sauté pan until it starts to sizzle. Add Seasoned Grapes and let cook for about 2–3 minutes. Add the wine and bring to a boil. Let the juice reduce by almost half. At this point add the 2 tbsp of butter cubes, shaking the pan back and forth to whip the sauce. You can do this when skewers are almost done.

FOR THE PRESENTATION

6 Serve with sautéed black cabbage on bottom of the plate. If you cannot find black cabbage, it's okay to use savoy cabbage instead. Lay 2 skewers of meat and potatoes on top. Pour the sauce over all

WINE PAIRING '01 BOTTEGA VINAIA LAGREIN

CARNE — SERVES 4

Petto di Pollo Ripieno con Funghi Assortiti e Formaggio Locale

STUFFED CHICKEN WITH FALL WILD MUSHROOMS AND FARM CHEESE

What a great combination of some of my favorite things! I grew up with chickens and I know chickens pretty well. In this dish we use only the breasts, which is my "Americanization" of the dish because the Americans love the chicken breast! I have stuffed a surprise filling of wild mushrooms that have an earthy taste which is bound to the smoothness of creamy farm cheese. The side of porcini bread pudding will make your mushroom lovers very happy!

For the Stuffing

1 lb assorted mushrooms, sliced
¼ cup olive oil
1 tsp garlic, chopped
salt and pepper
1½ cups farm cheese or substitute soft farmers cheese
½ cup Parmigiano Reggiano cheese
4 5-6 oz chicken breasts
1 egg
½ cup olive oil
all-purpose flour, for dredging
Porcini Bread Pudding (see recipe below)
Truffle Veloute (see following page)

For the Porcini Bread Pudding

1 cup dry porcini
1 tbsp butter
1 tbsp onion, chopped
1 cup heavy cream
2 eggs
½ tsp salt
pinch of black pepper
2 cups stale bread, crusts removed, diced in small cubes
4 4 oz metal timbales

FOR THE STUFFING

1 Sauté the mushrooms in the olive oil and garlic, then season with salt and pepper.

2 When they are done, let them cool on a tray. Add cheeses and egg when mushrooms are chilled. Set aside.

3 Take breast of chickens and trim of excess fat. Cut a pocket on the side of the breast, wide enough to be able to fill with 2 oz of stuffing.

4 Preheat oven to 450°F.

5 Have a sauté pan on the stove and heat about ½ cup of olive oil.

6 Dredge chicken breasts in flour, and then sear both sides until they are golden in color. Lay them on a baking sheet and finish baking them in the oven for about 20 minutes.

FOR THE PORCINI BREAD PUDDING

7 Soak the porcini mushrooms in 2 cups of hot water. Let them soak for about 10 minutes. Squeeze out the water and reserve for the truffle sauce.

8 Chop the mushrooms up and set aside.

9 Heat the butter in a pan. Add the onion and cook until just translucent. Add in the porcini mushrooms and some of the porcini water, about ½ cup. Be careful not to allow sediment from mushrooms to get into pan. Bring to a simmer and cook for another 10 minutes. Cool, then purée.

10 When they are ready, combine the mushrooms in a bowl with the rest of the ingredients.

11 Coat timbales with cooking spray. Fill about ¾ full with bread cubes in each timbale. Ladle in about ¼ cup of the porcini custard mix. Let this soak in for a couple of minutes and continue to add in a little more, almost to the edge.

12 Place the timbales in a water bath (see page 15).

13 Bake in a preheated 350°F oven until firm, about 30 minutes.

For the Truffle Veloute

1½ cups porcini water or vegetable stock
2 oz roux (2 tbsp butter cooked with 2 tbsp flour)
salt and pepper
½ cup heavy cream
2 tbsp truffle oil, white

The Porcini Bread Pudding and Tuffle Veloute can be made ahead and reheated.

FOR THE TRUFFLE VELOUTE

14 Bring the porcini water or stock to a boil. Add the roux and stir with a whisk. Continue to simmer for at least 15 minutes. Add the salt and pepper and heavy cream and simmer for another 5 minutes. When the sauce is ready, pour in the truffle oil. Stir.

FOR THE PRESENTATION

15 Remove bread pudding from timbale and place on side of plate. Choose a bright vegetable, like broccoli or purple kale to complement the dish and put adjacent to the timbale. Lean the chicken up against the broccoli and pour Truffle Veloute over all.

WINE PAIRING '98 PELISSERO BARBERA D'ALBA "PIANI"

2 tbsp butter
20 large sea scallops, previously coated in mushroom "powder" (see page 99)
½ cup Beurre Blanc (see page 76)
¼ cup wine
salt and pepper
1 lb cabbage, sliced or 2 cups cooked squash (see page 98)

PESCE — SERVES 4

Capesante in Crosta di Funghi

MUSHROOM CRUSTED SCALLOPS

This is a very easy and quick recipe. I'm using the same process as I do for the crusted shrimp appetizer. This is for mushroom lovers! Serve it with Porcini Bread Pudding [see page 122] and go crazy!

Some roast squash or cabbage would complement this dish very well.

1 Melt butter in a large pan. When it's hot, add the scallops. Cook on one side for about 2 minutes, and then turn them to cook a couple more minutes. Drain the excess grease. Season with salt and pepper.

2 Add the wine, let evaporate, and then add the Beurre Blanc. Bring it all to a gentle boil. They are done!

WINE PAIRING '04 COSTA DI BUSSIA CHARDONNAY

For the Leek Sauce

2 leeks, washed, trimmed and cut into small dice
¼ cup olive oil
1 quart vegetable stock
salt and pepper
4 tbsp butter

For the Procedure

1 cup dried porcini (soaked in hot water until soft)
¼ cup olive oil
2 tbsp onion, diced small
4 7 oz pieces lamb loins or lamb filet
salt and pepper
4 pieces frozen phyllo sheets, 9 x 6 inches
2 tbsp melted butter
1 lb black cabbage

Agnello con i Porcini in Crosta Fillo

SEASONAL LAMB LOIN WITH PORCINI AND LEEKS IN PHYLLO CRUST

You will find many of my recipes involve putting foods in packages formed from phyllo, parchment paper and puff pastry. I also enjoy cooking many stuffed meats and poultry. It is all variations of the traditional foods I grew up with, but I put my "twist" on it. In these foods, it is so much fun to have a surprise as you take that first bite!

FOR THE LEEK SAUCE

1 Heat oil in pot and sauté leeks. Let cook until it is tender. Add the stock and seasoning. Let cook for 10 more minutes. Purée all with an immersion blender until smooth.

2 Pour the sauce in a sauté pan. Bring to a boil. Add the butter in small quantities to obtain a thick sauce. Take a final taste to adjust seasoning.

FOR THE PROCEDURE

3 Drain porcini from water, reserving the water for later.

4 Sauté the onion in the olive oil until translucent. Add the mushrooms and let cook for about 5-6 minutes. Add a little of the porcini water to keep them soft, being careful not to pour in the sediment from the mushrooms. Purée all in the food processor and let cool.

5 Meanwhile, sear the lamb loin in a pan with some hot oil. Season lightly with salt and pepper. Using a table knife spread the porcini purée all over the lamb loin.

6 Lay out phyllo sheets. Brush each one with melted butter, keeping it on the horizontal side. Lay loin in and wrap up just like you would be making a package. Do the same on the sides, folding the edges in. Turn over and brush the top with butter and place on a baking tray.

7 Bake in a preheated 450°F oven. Bake until phyllo is golden brown.

FOR THE PRESENTATION

8 Cut each lamb loin on a bias and serve with the Leek Sauce and sautéed black cabbage.

WINE PAIRING '02 CASTELLO DI CORBARA LAGO DI CORBARA

For the Panna Cotta

1 cup heavy cream
1 tsp brown sugar
1 tsp granulated sugar
1 gelatin sheet
splash of vanilla extract
½ cup canned pumpkin
pinch of ground cinnamon
pinch of ground cloves
pinch of ground ginger
pinch of ground nutmeg

Candied Pecans (see recipe below)
Powdered sugar

For the Candied Pecans

1½ cups pecan halves
1 egg white
2 tbsp sugar
½ tsp ground cinnamon
½ tsp ground ginger
½ tsp ground nutmeg
½ tsp ground cloves

DOLCE — SERVES 4

Panna Cotta alla Zucca con Noci Candite

PUMPKIN PANNA COTTA WITH CANDIED PECANS

Gelatin sheets work much better than powdered gelatin, but they might be hard to find. Try a specialty store. If you need to use powdered gelatin, you will need 1/4 oz.

Any extra pecans could be served with coffee or tea—as a treat!

FOR THE PANNA COTTA

1 Bring heavy cream and sugars to a simmer in medium saucepan over medium heat.

2 If using gelatin sheets, soften in cold water and lightly wring out.

3 Remove cream from heat and whisk in gelatin, vanilla, pumpkin and spices.

4 Pour into four, 4 oz timbales or ramekins. Refrigerate until set.

FOR THE CANDIED PECANS

6 Preheat oven to 350°F.

7 Coarsely chop pecans and set aside in large bowl.

8 Mix sugar, cinnamon, ginger, nutmeg and cloves thoroughly in a separate bowl.

9 Whisk egg whites in separate bowl just until frothy. Pour egg whites over pecan pieces and toss with hands until all pieces are completely covered.

10 Add ½ of sugar mixture over pecans and toss until all pieces are completely coated. Repeat with the remaining sugar mixture.

11 Spread mixture out onto well-sprayed sheet tray. *Do not* use parchment paper.

12 Bake for about 5 minutes, and then stir pecans around. Bake for another 5–8 minutes or until pecans have dried out and sugar mixture has become a crisp coating. Keep a close eye on them, so they don't burn! Cool completely at room temperature.

13 Store in a cool dry place.

FOR THE PRESENTATION

14 Unmold Panna cotta in the center of the plate (see page 15). Place pecans around it and lightly sprinkle with powdered sugar. Garnish with fresh mint.

WINE PAIRING NV DABARTOLI "VECCHIO SAMPERI"

For the Crepes

2 eggs
¾ cup bread flour
1 cup whole milk
1 tbsp granulated sugar

For the Apple Slices

3 Granny Smith apples
¼ cup brown sugar
2 tbsp butter, melted

To Assemble

1 cup amaretto cookies, crushed like sand
Caramel Sauce (see recipe below)

For the Caramel Sauce

1 cup sugar
1 cup lemon juice
2 cups heavy cream

DOLCE — YIELD 1 STACKED CAKE

"Millefoglie" di Crespelle alle Mele

APPLE CREPE STACK

Millefoglie literally means "thousand leaves." It's a typical dessert made usually with layered puff pastry, vanilla custard and chocolate custard—lots of powdered sugar on top. In this case, I used the word millefoglie because of the concept of how dessert is assembled.

Any extra crepes can be stored in the freezer for future use.

FOR THE CREPES

1 In a large bowl whisk together the eggs and flour, then gradually add the milk. Continue to stir to prevent lumps. Pour through a strainer and stir in sugar.

2 If you are skilled, heat 2 crepe pans, spray them and use a 2 oz ladle, not quite full of batter, to transfer the batter to the pans. Flip the crepes after a minute or so and let the other side get some color. Otherwise, use 1 pan, it will just take you a little longer.

3 Transfer to a sheet tray with paper. Continue until all the batter is used.

FOR THE APPLE SLICES

4 Peel and core the apples, then slice them very thinly. Toss the slices with the melted butter and brown sugar. Spread them evenly on a sprayed sheet tray and bake at 350°F for about 10 minutes, until the slices are soft but not mushy. Let cool.

TO ASSEMBLE

5 Place 1 crepe on a plate, cover with a layer of apple slices, sprinkle well with cookie crumbs then top with another crepe, apple slices, etc. until all the 6 crepes are used. The uppermost layer is a crepe, not apple slices.

FOR THE CARAMEL SAUCE

6 Combine sugar and lemon juice in a pot. Stir with a wooden spoon until sugar has dissolved and mixture becomes a nice golden syrup.

7 Add the heavy cream. Caramel will clump together; don't worry, it's still okay!

8 Keep on the stove, always stirring until the clumps dissolve and the sauce has boiled for 2–3 minutes.

FOR THE PRESENTATION

9 Cut stack into 6 portions. Warm up slightly and serve with whipped cream and caramel sauce.

WINE PAIRING '98 MACULAN TORCOLATO

DOLCE — YIELD 1 CAKE

Torta di Mele

APPLE CAKE WITH VANILLA CREAM SAUCE

For the Cake

- 1½ cups vegetable oil
- 2 cups granulated sugar
- 3 eggs
- 3 cups all-purpose flour
- 1½ tsp baking soda
- ¼ tsp ground ginger
- ½ tsp ground cinnamon
- ½ tsp salt
- 1 lb Granny Smith apples, peeled, cored and chopped
- 1 cup raisins
- Vanilla Cream Sauce (see recipe below)

For Vanilla Cream Sauce

- 2 cups heavy cream
- 4 egg yolks
- ½ cup sugar
- 1 vanilla bean or 1 tsp vanilla extract

FOR THE CAKE

1 Preheat oven to 325°F. Spray a 10-inch spring-form pan.

2 In the bowl of a mixer, beat the oil and sugar for about 5 minutes. Add the eggs, one at a time.

3 In another bowl, sift together the dry ingredients. Stir this gradually into the wet ingredients, adding the apples and raisins at the end.

4 Pour into prepared pan and bake 1½-2 hours, until skewer inserted in the center comes out clean.

5 Serve with Vanilla Cream Sauce or fresh whipped cream.

FOR VANILLA CREAM SAUCE

6 Bring cream to a boil. Add vanilla bean. When cream boils, split and scrape vanilla bean into milk. Discard pod.

7 In a separate pan, mix egg yolk and sugar. Add milk mixture with a whisk.

8 Then, put on a low heat and using a wooden spoon continue stirring. Do not allow to boil. It will thicken.

WINE PAIRING NV DE BARTOLI "VECCHIO SAMPERI"

8 tbsp unsalted butter, softened
½ cup sugar
1 egg
¼ cup chocolate powder
1 cup all-purpose flour
White Chocolate Hazelnut Mousse (see page 132)
Chocolate Sauce (see page 132)

DOLCE — YIELDS 22-24 COOKIES

Panini di Biscotti al Cacao

COCOA COOKIE SANDWICHES

1 Cream together the butter and sugar, then add the egg. Fold in the chocolate and flour. Refrigerate dough until firm.

2 Divide dough into 2, placing one half between 2 sheets of plastic wrap, roll out to about ¼-inch thickness. Place on sheet tray and refrigerate until firm. Repeat process with second half of dough.

3 Remove the first tray of dough and cut out cookies with desired cookie cutter. Place on sheet tray lined with parchment paper. Repeat with 2nd tray and with dough scraps that are leftover. Bake at 350°F for 10 minutes.

WINE PAIRING '98 VILLA LA SELVA VIN SANTO "VIGNA DEL PAPA"

For the Mousse

- 1½ cups heavy cream
- 1½ cups mascarpone cheese
- ½ cup White Chocolate Syrup – Torani
- ½ cup hazelnuts, toasted and chopped
- powdered sugar

For the Chocolate Sauce

- 1½ cups heavy cream
- ½ cup chocolate chips
- 1 tbsp honey

DOLCE – YIELDS 11-12 SANDWICH COOKIES

Mousse al Cioccolato Bianco e Nocciole e Salsa al Cioccolato

WHITE CHOCOLATE HAZELNUT MOUSSE AND CHOCOLATE SAUCE

I'm sure you will say: "Where the heck can I find white chocolate syrup?" Well, in case you are having a hard time, just substitute with 1 cup white chocolate. Remember, you will need to melt it in a double boiler!

FOR THE MOUSSE

1 Whip cream to soft peaks. Place in separate bowl.

2 On low speed whip mascarpone with white chocolate syrup. Whipping on a high speed will cause the mascarpone to separate.

3 Mix in hazelnuts and fold in whipped cream.

FOR THE CHOCOLATE SAUCE

4 Bring the cream to a boil. Take it off the stove and add the chocolate and honey. Stir until the chocolate is melted and well-mixed. Pour it into a container until ready to serve.

FOR THE PRESENTATION

5 Place mousse between 2 cookies, then put 2-3 cookies on each plate and drizzle with chocolate sauce and powdered sugar.

- ½ cup chocolate powder
- ¾ all purpose flour
- 1 cup granulated sugar
- 2¼ cups whole milk
- ¾ cup chocolate chips
- ½ tsp vanilla extract
- ½ tsp ground cinnamon

DOLCE — SERVES 5

Budino al Cioccolato con Cannella

CINNAMON CHOCOLATE PUDDING

By now, you know a Budino is a pudding!

1 Mix the chocolate powder, flour and sugar in a mixing bowl.

2 Slowly whisk in a little of the milk to form a paste. Add the remaining milk to make a thin batter. Transfer to a large saucepan and heat over medium heat while stirring constantly until it begins to boil. Simmer 10 minutes while stirring.

3 Remove from heat and add the chocolate chips, vanilla and cinnamon. Stir to mix well.

4 After the chocolate is completely melted, pour into five, 5 oz timbales or ramekins to about ⅘ full.

5 Chill and sprinkle with toasted pine nuts, if desired.

WINE PAIRING '00 PERUINI "PRIMO AMORE"

1 lb Challah bread, cubed
4½ cups whole milk
1½ cups sugar
1½ lbs canned pumpkin
6 eggs, beaten
Caramel Sauce (see page 128)
powdered sugar

DOLCE — SERVES 12

Budino di Pane alla Zucca

PUMPKIN CHALLAH BREAD PUDDING

This is great with caramel sauce and fresh whipped cream!

A Budino is a pudding!

1 Spray a 9 x 5 inch loaf pan and sprinkle with sugar. Put cubed bread in it.

2 Heat together the milk, sugar and pumpkin purée until almost boiling. Remove from heat and let cool.

3 Stir in the eggs, being careful not to scramble them.

4 Pour mixture slowly over the bread, making sure the bread soaks up the liquid. Let sit for 20 minutes.

5 Take 9 x 5 inch loaf pan and place in water bath (see page 15). Cover all with tin foil. Bake in 350°F oven for 2 hours, removing tin foil for the last 30 minutes of baking.

6 Chill before removing from the pan and cutting. Sprinkle with powdered sugar and serve with caramel sauce.

WINE PAIRING '01 MACULAN "DINDARELLO"

It is the smell of winter that I remember so clearly growing up in Italy. We definitely spent lots of time in the house baking cakes and cookies [I have a sweet tooth] and drinking lots of tea. My nonna always had a treat for us and made us an Italian drink called Vin Brulé, hot red wine with sugar, cinnamon sticks, orange zest, and cloves. My mamma made stew and slow cooked foods, usually made with pork and the whole house would fill with this great smell, true comfort food.

We never had lots of snow in Trissino. I remember just two or three big snowstorms in my childhood. One thing that always will be part of my memories is this treat that my mamma made for my sorella Graziella and me. A glass filled with fresh snow, red wine and sugar! I can still taste it in my mouth.

inverno

WINTER

For the Braised Oxtail

- 7 lbs oxtail
- ½ cup olive oil
- 1 tsp salt
- ½ tsp pepper
- 1 carrot, cut into small dice
- 3 stalks celery, cut into small dice
- 1 small onion, cut into small dice
- 5 garlic cloves, peeled
- 1½ cups red wine
- 1 sprig fresh rosemary
- 1 bunch fresh sage
- 5 cups water
- 1 can diced tomatoes (16 oz)
- ¼ cup tomato puree

For the Napoléon

- 1 package frozen phyllo dough
- 2 tbsp melted butter
- 1 cup shavings of Pecorino Romano cheese
- black pepper

ANTIPASTO — SERVES 6

Sfoglia con Coda di Bue e Pecorino

PHYLLO NAPOLEON WITH SHREDDED, BRAISED OXTAIL & PECORINO CHEESE

The longer I have been at Paesano's the more I have earned the trust of our customers. It is because of this trust that I like to put one item on the menu that is a little "out there", like kidney, snail, tripe, pork bones. And this oxtail! This recipe will give you about 1 1/2 lbs of cooked pulled meat. It's definitely a big batch of stew. Remember, you can always freeze in small batches for future use. It will take some time between the cooking and the final stage of pulling the meat off the bone and making the sauce.

To make cheese shavings I find it very easy using a simple carrot peeler! To prevent the Napoléon from sliding on the plate, put some sauce on the bottom before laying the phyllo or use some lettuce leaves as a garnish "bed".

FOR THE BRAISED OXTAIL

1 Heat a wide, low braising pot. Add the oil then add the meat. Brown it on both sides and season with salt and pepper.

2 Add vegetables and cook for a few minutes. Pour in red wine and let it evaporate. Add tomato purée, diced tomatoes, and water. Bring to a slow simmer. It will take 3–4 hours. The meat will be so tender it will come off the bone! At this point, take the meat from the pot and place in a pan to cool a little.

3 Meanwhile, go through the sauce, discarding rosemary and sage and any bones left behind.

4 Using a food processor or immersion blender purée the sauce until it's all smooth. Taste and adjust with salt and pepper. (A potato masher also works, just be sure to separate the liquid from the vegetables, as it will make it easier to mash.)

5 When the meat is cool enough to handle, start pulling it off the bones, discarding the fat too. Purée any sauce left over on the bottom of the pan, and add it to the rest. Add the meat to the sauce and mix.

FOR THE NAPOLÉON

6 Preheat the oven to 350°F.

7 Lay the sheet of phyllo on the table. Cut into squares of 4 x 4 inches. You will need 3 squares per portion.

8 Display on a baking sheet. Brush all phyllo with the butter and sprinkle with pepper. Bake until golden brown in color, about 15–20 minutes.

FOR THE PRESENTATION

9 Lay one piece of phyllo on the plate, cover with about ¼ cup of meat and sauce and sprinkle with Pecorino Romano shavings. Add one more layer of phyllo and repeat again with the meat and cheese. Finish with one more layer of phyllo.

WINE PAIRING '03 CAPUTO AGLIANICO SANNIO "CLANIUS"

60 mussels, washed and de-bearded
½ cup extra virgin olive oil
1–2 tbsp extra virgin olive oil
8 oz bacon cut into thin strips about 3 x ⅛ inches
1 onion, julienned
8 oz roasted peppers, store bought
1 tsp red pepper flakes
slices of sourdough bread

ANTIPASTO — SERVES 4

Cozze all'Amatriciana

SPICY SEASONAL MUSSELS APPETIZER

"Amatriciana" means from the city of Amatrice. In any recipe that is cooked all'Amatriciana you will always find some element of pork. Here I use bacon. It's a very easy appetizer!

If you don't have a wide enough pan to hold all the mussels at once, it's okay. You can try using two pans, a little tricky, or just make two batches.

1 Heat the oil in a wide sauté pan. Add mussels. Cover with a lid and let mussels open up. Keep a bowl on the side so you can put the open mussels whenever they are ready.

2 When all the mussels are open, pour leftover juice on top. Using the same pan add 1–2 tablespoons of olive oil and the bacon and let cook until it starts to get crispy. Add onions and cook all together.

FOR THE PRESENTATION

3 Finally add peppers and flakes. When it is time to serve, divide mussels into 4 pasta bowls. Pour the juice back in the pan with the rest of the ingredients. Bring to a quick boil. Pour in the middle of each pasta bowl. Serve with toasted or grilled bread.

WINE PAIRING '04 FONTALEONI VERNACCIA DI SAN GEMIGNANO

Pasta con Salsa Pevarada

WAVY PASTA WITH TRADITIONAL PEVARADA

For the Sauce

- 3 tbsp onion, cut into small dice
- 2 tbsp butter
- 4 filets of anchovies
- 1 lb chicken liver, trimmed of excess fat, cut in small dice
- 8 oz salami, cut into ½-inch cubes
- 1 cup white wine
- 2 tbsp veal glaze
- 3 tbsp fresh parsley, finely chopped
- ½ tsp pepper
- ½ tsp salt
- 1 lb dried pasta, Mafaldine if available
- Parmigiano Reggiano cheese

Salsa Pevarada originated in the city of Treviso and appears in a fourteenth-century Veneto cookbook. The sauce is for chicken liver lovers and also tastes great with roasted meats and guinea fowl.

The pasta used in this appetizer is Mafaldine, long flat ribbons of pasta with crinkly edges. It's a dry product, available in specialty stores. I use the Voiello brand. If you cannot find this kind and shape, you can use any other dry or fresh pasta.

Veal glaze is available in most gourmet stores. If unavailable add some beef base or chicken base and taste before adding salt to the sauce!

FOR THE SAUCE

1 Cook the onion with the butter until transparent. Add the anchovies and stir occasionally until they dissolve.

2 Add liver and let cook for 5–6 minutes. Pour in the wine and veal glaze. Cook slowly for another 10 minutes.

3 Remove from stove and add chopped parsley, salt and pepper to taste. Use immediately or store in a container for a few days in the refrigerator.

4 Prepare the pasta according to directions on package. Drain. Toss with sauce and sprinkle with cheese.

WINE PAIRING '01 VIETTI NEBBIOLO "PERBACCO"

For the Fennel Custard

- 2 fresh fennel bulbs
- 1 tbsp olive oil
- 2 tbsp onion, chopped
- pinch of salt and pepper
- ½ cup heavy cream
- 4 egg yolks
- ½ tsp salt
- pinch of pepper
- pan spray
- 4 4 oz timbales or ramekins

For the Salad

- 2 blood oranges or regular oranges
- 5 oz smoked bay scallops
- 2 tbsp extra virgin olive oil
- ½ tsp salt
- ¼ tsp black pepper

ANTIPASTO — SERVES 4

Budino di Finocchio con Capesante Affumicate ed Arance

FENNEL CUSTARD, SMOKED BAY SCALLOPS & BLOOD ORANGE SALAD

Definitely a different way to serve the classic combination of orange and fennel.

FOR THE FENNEL CUSTARD

1 Clean the fennel down to the bulb. Cut, core and small dice it. You should have at least 1 lb of fennel to continue.

2 Heat the oil in pan and sauté the onion until translucent. Add the fennel and stir. Add salt and pepper. Continue to cook until the fennel is tender. Remove from heat and purée.

3 When cooled, slowly combine 1 cup of the fennel purée with remaining 4 ingredients. Mix well.

4 Spray timbales to coat. Fill them to the top with the fennel custard mix. Place them in baking pan half filled with water. Bake them for 30–40 minutes in a 350°F preheated oven. Remove from the oven and cool.

5 The custard can be used the same day; just reheat slightly in oven for 15-20 more minutes or cover each one in plastic wrap and refrigerate.

FOR THE SALAD

6 Cut off both ends of the orange. Using a skinny, sharp knife, cut off the skin, following the round shape of the orange. Make sure to get the white pith off. At this point you should have a skinless orange. Hold orange in one hand and use knife to cut wedges in between the thin white skin. If you do this the right way, you will be left with the inside white part only. Squeeze excess juice from it in a bowl with the wedges. Add scallops. Stir in seasonings. Toss all together.

FOR THE PRESENTATION

7 Remove custard from ramekins onto 4 appetizer plates. If you have difficulty removing custard, quickly dip the bottoms of the ramekins or timbales in hot water to loosen the custard, then turn over onto plate. Lay the salad all around it. Garnish with some herbs and/or some radicchio leaves. Sprinkle custard with mixed ground pepper.

WINE PAIRING '04 CAVALCHINA BIANCO DI CUSTOZA

2 cups watercress, de-stemmed
2 cups radicchio and endive mix (1 small radicchio, half bunch curly endive)
1 fennel bulb, thinly sliced
8 oz feta cheese, cut in small cubes
1 cup honey roasted almonds (see recipe below)
6–7 oz Blood Orange Dressing (see recipe below)
1 cup mandarin orange slices

For Honey Roasted Almonds
1 cup blanched almonds, slivered
3 tbsp honey

For Blood Orange Syrup
2 cups sugar
1 cup water
juice of 2 blood oranges

For Blood Orange Dressing
½ cup Blood Orange Syrup (see recipe below)
½ cup olive oil
3 tbsp white vinegar
3 tbsp chilled water
pinch of salt and pepper

INSALATA — SERVES 4

Insalata Siciliana Invernale

WINTER SICILIAN SALAD

FOR BLOOD ORANGE SYRUP

1 Heat water and sugar until they reach a boil. Add juice of oranges. Let cool.

FOR BLOOD ORANGE DRESSING

2 Put all ingredients together in deep container and mix using immersion blender.

FOR HONEY ROASTED ALMONDS

3 Put the almonds in a small bowl. Toss them with the honey and then spread them out onto a full sized sheet pan.

4 Bake at 350°F for 10–15 minutes. Stir occasionally during baking to prevent burning.

5 Remove from oven and continue to stir while they cool. When cool, they may be stored in covered container.

FOR THE PRESENTATION

6 Mix first 4 salad ingredients together. Toss with the salad dressing and sprinkle with almonds. Top with thin orange slices.

WINE PAIRING '04 CASTELVERO CORTESE

For the Kidney

8 tbsp butter (1 stick)
2 large shallots, cut into thin slices
1½ lbs kidney, cleaned and cut into slices ¼-inch thick
all-purpose flour, for dredging
salt and pepper to taste
½ cup brandy
2 tbsp Italian parsley, chopped
8 small slices Polenta (see recipe below)

For the Polenta

3½ cups of water
1 tsp salt
2 tbsp extra virgin olive oil
¾ cup polenta
2 tbsp Parmigiano Reggiano cheese

ANTIPASTO — SERVES 4

Rognoni di Vitello in Padella

SAUTÉED VEAL KIDNEY WITH BRANDY & GRILLED POLENTA

I love kidneys! It was one of my favorite foods when I was growing up and I make it just like my mamma! Grilled polenta is another dish I ate growing up. I can picture my family sitting at the table with a big flat of polenta on the table and maybe a little stew of something, probably pork and that would be dinner. We would live on polenta!

Cleaning kidney is not a bad job, but if you are not willing to do it, ask your butcher to do it for you. If you are willing to try, take off the fat found in the center of the kidney. Cut it in the middle lengthwise and then with a small boning knife [skinny and pointed] take off the fat. Kidney, especially this small, cooks very quickly, so keep this in mind to avoid overcooking it.

Padella simply means sauté pan!

FOR THE KIDNEY

1 In a large sauté pan, add 4 tablespoons of butter and let melt; add shallots and cook until almost translucent. Meanwhile toss kidney in the flour to coat, shaking off excess. Add kidney to the pan. Keep flame on high so it will sear the food very well. Add salt and pepper. Pour brandy and watch out for any flame! Let it evaporate completely. Add leftover butter, shaking the pan back and forth to give it a thick consistency. Sprinkle with parsley and serve with polenta.

FOR THE POLENTA

2 Bring water to boil with salt and oil. Turn heat down to simmer and add the polenta slowly while stirring. Continue cooking and stirring for about 30 more minutes.

3 Remove from heat and stir in the cheese. Set aside.

4 Spray large sheet pan (10 x 13 inches). Pour out the polenta onto the tray and smooth out using a spatula. Cover with a sheet of parchment or plastic wrap and let cool.

5 Cut polenta into desired sizes and brush with some butter and sprinkle with cheese. Grill or bake in 450°F preheated oven for 20 minutes or until golden in color.

FOR THE PRESENTATION

6 Place kidney in soup bowl with sauce. Lay slices of polenta along side.

WINE PAIRING '03 BADIA A COLTIBUONO CHIANTI CLASSICO "RS"

½ tbsp vegetable bouillon base or already prepared vegetable stock
2 tbsp onion
1 tbsp olive oil
1 lb Arborio rice
salt
½ cup balsamic vinegar
½ cup Parmigiano Reggiano cheese, grated
1 oz butter
2 tbsp Italian parsley, finely chopped
1 egg
½ cup fresh breadcrumbs
½ cup olive oil
all-purpose flour, for coating
Balsamic Glaze (see page 176)

ANTIPASTO O CONTORO — SERVES 4

Polpette di Risotto al Balsamico

OVEN BAKED BALSAMIC AND PARMESAN RISOTTO CAKES

In the Veneto region, rice is more popular than pasta. It is grown in the humid, marshy areas of Northern Italy that provide ideal conditions. Besides Vicenza's famous Baccalà fish dish, it is also known for its risotto dish, risi e bisi, a spring risotto with rice and peas. In order to really enjoy risotto it must be eaten immediately after it is made to experience the creamy texture. If it is left to sit it will dry out and reheating makes it soft and mushy. I can't stand that! This is why you do not see it on the menu at Paesano's. I feel if I can't make it to be served perfectly I don't want to do it. So until I figure out how to do that, eating risotto cakes is a very good alternative! Here, you make the risotto, add breadcrumbs and eggs, and form them into patties for frying. I think you will find these quite delicious.

1 Combine the vegetable base with 2 quarts of hot water or use already prepared stock. Bring it to a boil.

2 Cook onion in oil until translucent. Add rice and stir with a wooden spoon until it is very, very hot. Season lightly with salt. Add balsamic vinegar and let evaporate until it is very dry. At this point add the stock a little at a time, enough to cover the rice. Always wait until it has been absorbed before adding more liquid. Risotto takes about 20 minutes to be done.

3 When it is done, remove from stove and add cheese, butter and parsley. Spread the mixture out on a sheet pan to cool.

4 When cool, scrape it all into a bowl and combine it with the egg and breadcrumbs. Mix well.

5 Using an ice cream scoop, scoop out balls of the mixture on a half sheet pan and flatten them slightly to make them look like cakes. Cover with plastic wrap.

6 When ready to use, heat enough oil to be able to pan fry the cakes in 2 large sauté pans. Flour rice cakes on both sides, then sear them on both sides until they look colored and crispy. Pat them on paper towel to remove excess grease.

FOR THE PRESENTATION

7 Display on a serving platter. Drizzle with Balsamic Glaze.

WINE PAIRING '02 AIA VECCHIA "LAGONE"

Risotto

Most famous for its risotto is Vicenza. Every family has its own version of the specialty risi e bisi, spring peas with risotto. When the first sweetest spring peas arrive is when risi e bisi is at its best. Since Vicenza is also noted for its vegetables, it is also common to see risotto made with every vegetable imaginable, from asparagus and fennel in the spring to wild mushrooms, pumpkin and squashes in the fall.

When made properly risotto is cooked slowly, first sautéing onion and butter, then adding the rice and mixing it well in the pan. You must constantly stir the risotto as you gradually add stock just to cover the rice. Wait for it to be absorbed before adding more stock. Tasting it to assure it is cooked perfectly is the key and then adding Parmigiano Reggiano. The final rule of risotto making is to end with butter. The result will be a delicious creaminess that covers every grain.

Risotto takes 20 minutes to be ready. You cook it, you serve it, you eat it! That's it!

PASTA — SERVES 4

Pasta con Tonno Grigliato

GRILLED TUNA & MALFADINE PASTA & LEMON ARTICHOKE PESTO

For the Procedure

- 12 oz dry pasta, malfadine or pasta of your choice, cooked according to directions
- 3 skewers of 5 oz cubed tuna, grilled or seared in pan
- 1 cup pitted black kalamata olives
- 4 tbsp capers
- 1 cup Lemon Artichoke Pesto (see recipe below)
- 4 tbsp extra virgin olive oil

For the Lemon Artichoke Pesto

- 12 oz canned artichoke hearts, quartered and drained
- 8 tbsp pine nuts, toasted
- ½ cup Parmigiano Reggiano cheese
- 3 tbsp Italian parsley, finely chopped
- 1 lemon, zested and juiced
- ½ tsp salt
- ¼ tsp pepper
- ½ cup extra virgin olive oil

This is another pretty easy recipe to prepare. To make it even easier, you could partially grill the tuna earlier in the day to get the flavor and then add it to the pan. If it's too cold to grill the tuna outside, you could sear it in the pan before adding all the ingredients.

When draining the pasta, always reserve some cooking water in case the pasta will be too dry with the sauce.

It will save you time if you prepare the pesto the day before.

FOR THE PROCEDURE

1 While the pasta cooks, prepare the sauce.

2 Heat the oil; add olives and capers to warm through. Add tuna (removed from the skewers) and Lemon Artichoke Pesto. Toss all together.

FOR THE LEMON ARTICHOKE PESTO

3 Using a food processor grind up the artichokes. Slowly add in the pine nuts and cheese. After it is ground smooth, scrape mixture into a large bowl and add the remaining ingredients. Mix well. Put in a covered container until ready to use.

FOR THE PRESENTATION

4 Divide pasta into 4 plates. Place reserved tuna on pasta. Drizzle extra sauce on top and garnish with capers and olives.

WINE PAIRING '04 CUSUMANO "ANGIMBE"

16 oz Oxtail Stew (see page 138)
Pecorino Romano cheese

For the Winter Gnocchi
3 lbs russet potatoes
2 cups all-purpose flour
1 large egg
1 tsp salt

PASTA — SERVES 6

Gnocchi di Patate con Coda di Bue

WINTER GNOCCHI WITH OXTAIL STEW

The gnocchi here are the potato or winter gnocchi, different than the ricotta gnocchi in the summer section and the gnudi in the fall section. Gnocchi are served with a wide variety of sauces. For this dish we are using the oxtail sauce previously made for the appetizer.

Gnocchi might be a little difficult to prepare. The dough could be a little sticky so you must be able to judge if you need more or less flour to get the right consistency. It should be soft, but not sticky. I always cook a little dough in boiling water to see how the consistency is, then I go ahead with the recipe. The more you do it, the better you will become at judging when it is just right. So, don't be afraid to try.

FOR THE WINTER GNOCCHI

1 Place the whole potatoes in a saucepan with warm water to cover. Bring to a boil and cook at a low boil until they are soft, about 45 minutes. Cool slightly and while still warm, peel the potatoes and pass them through a vegetable mill or ricer onto a clean pasta board or cutting board.

2 Make a well in the center of the potatoes and sprinkle all over with flour. Break the egg in the center of the well, add the salt and using a fork, stir into the flour and potatoes as if you were making pasta. Once the egg is mixed in, bring the dough together, kneading gently until a ball is formed. Continue kneading gently for another 4 minutes or until the ball is dry to the touch.

3 Divide the dough into 6 large balls. Roll each ball into ¾-inch cylinders and cut the cylinders into 1-inch pieces.

4 Use a dinner fork to shape the gnocchi. Hold the fork in front of you with the concave side down. Take one piece of dough and using your opposite thumb press it against the tips of the tines and flick it away. You should end up with a ridge on one side and a depression on the other.

5 Cook the gnocchi as you would cook any pasta. They will be ready when they float. Use a strainer, taking gnocchi out whenever they are ready.

FOR THE PRESENTATION

6 Reheat the oxtail stew. When gnocchi are ready toss them with the sauce.

7 Divide into 4 pasta bowls or serve the stew family style on a platter. Sprinkle with shavings of Pecorino Romano cheese.

WINE PAIRING '01 PAOLO BEA MONTEFALCO ROSSO RISERVA

- 1¾ lbs stale bread, cubed
- 1¼ quarts whole milk
- ¾ lb frozen spinach
- 1 oz unsalted butter
- pinch of ground nutmeg
- pinch of salt and pepper
- 2 tsp extra virgin olive oil
- ½ small onion, diced
- 2 eggs
- ½ cup Pecorino Romano cheese
- 1 cup bread flour
- 1 tsp salt
- 1 cup Parmigiano Reggiano cheese, grated
- 3 tbsp butter, melted
- ¼ cup fresh sage, chopped

PASTA — SERVES 6

Strangolapreti

PRIESTCHOKERS

This dish has been a great success at Paesano's. We put it back on the winter menu because people kept asking for it. These are very good eaten topped with grated cheese and melted butter as in the recipe, or you can add Breaded Baked Shrimp [see page 59] as we serve them in the restaurant. Many people ask about the name. It comes from the folklore that reminds us of a glutinous priest who was eating these delicious "dumplings" too quickly and choked. So enjoy every bite, slowly!

1 Soak the cubed bread in the milk for at least 30 minutes.

2 Defrost the spinach and squeeze out all the excess water.

3 Melt the butter in a large sauté pan. Cook the spinach and season with the nutmeg, salt and pepper.

4 In another saucepan sauté the onions in olive oil until translucent.

5 Mash up the soaked bread and milk and then add the cooked spinach and onions. Add the eggs, cheese and the flour. Mix well by hand.

6 Using an ice cream scoop, make balls from the mixture and boil them in salted water. Remove from the boiling water when they float to the top. Scoop them onto a drain pan to cool. Refrigerate until ready to use.

7 Get a new pot of boiling, salted water. Drop dumplings into the water and boil for at least 4–5 minutes. You need to make sure they are hot all the way through.

FOR THE PRESENTATION

8 When ready, remove from water using a slotted spoon. Sprinkle heavily with cheese, drizzle with hot melted butter and fresh sage.

WINE PAIRING SCILIO ETNA ROSSO "RUBE"

24 oz pork liver, cut into slices about ½-inch thick, about 2 x 2 inches
1 lb caul fat, from pork (see pg 14)
1 lb shallots (about 8 or 9 whole shallots)
½ cup olive oil
salt and pepper
8–10 fresh sage leaves

CARNE — SERVES 4

Fegato di Maiale con il "radeselo"

NONNA SILVIA'S PORK LIVER WRAPPED IN CAUL FAT

I inserted this recipe, very easy, to honor my nonna, Silvia. At over 80 years old, she still has a great spirit and positive attitude, even though her health has been very shaky for the last 10 years. I believe my nonna had a very hard life, with 10 kids and most definitely not easy times. She is a great example of my "don't let yourself down kind of thing" as long as "la buona salute" [good health] is with you.

1 Cut caul fat into pieces at least twice the size of the liver slices, big enough to wrap each individual liver slices. Place liver on top of caul and fold like you would a package.

2 Cut shallot in julienne slices and cook in oil until translucent. Remove from pan.

3 Use the same pan to cook liver, about 2–3 minutes on each side. Season with salt and pepper. Add sage and then add shallots to season all together for a few minutes.

FOR THE PRESENTATION

4 Serve with polenta.

WINE PAIRING '03 BOROLI "ANNA"

I tre fratelli Nicoletti

- 1 whole chicken
- 2 celery stalks, diced
- 1 carrot, diced
- 1 onion, diced
- 1 fresh sprig rosemary
- 1 small bundle of fresh sage
- 3-4 garlic cloves, peeled and minced
- 2-3 bay leaves
- black peppercorn
- 1 bottle Chianti wine
- chicken stock

Pollo Arrosto al Chianti

CHIANTI WINE ROASTED CHICKEN

I used to help my mamma and papá with the killing, cleaning, cooking and of course the eating of our chickens. We used the whole chicken, even the intestines. My mamma would clean the intestines with vinegar and cooked them with tomato sauce. [That is how my nonna Giovanna used to make them. That's how I learned too.] Back when my papá was a kid, he ate the chicken feet too. In this recipe we use the whole cut up chicken — don't worry: no intestine, no feet!

This would be great to eat just as is, but at the restaurant we serve it with Pevarada Sauce [see page 141] and Potato Tortino [see page 156] as a side.

1 Cut chicken in half and each half in quarters. Your butcher may do this for you in the store.

2 Put chicken in a bowl and add celery, carrots, and onions. Add the rest of the ingredients, pouring the wine in last. Cover with plastic wrap and let it sit overnight in the refrigerator.

3 When ready to cook, drain the chicken from the liquid and pat dry. Strain wine from the vegetables and reserve it for the sauce.

4 Preheat the oven at 450°F. Warm up a large pan.

5 The idea is to cook all of the chicken in the pan and put it in the oven. If you don't have such large cookware, you could sear the chicken a little at a time in a smaller pan and then transfer it in a deep baking pan.

6 Add oil to the pan, dredge chicken in the flour and put in the pan on high heat, skin down first. Let cook for 2–3 minutes on each side to get a nice crispy look. Sprinkle with salt and pepper. Add half of reserved strained wine to the pan and let it partially evaporate. Put the pan in the oven and roast about 30–45 minutes until done.

7 Check on the chicken as it cooks to see if it needs more liquid. Add more wine or chicken stock so it does not dry out. Also turn chicken over halfway through the cooking time.

WINE PAIRING '03 VALDIPIATTA ROSSO DI MONTEPULCIANO

For the Cauliflower Sauce

1 whole cauliflower
1 quart whole milk
1 tsp salt
1 tsp pepper

For the Vegetable Topping

½ cup extra virgin olive oil
1 cup celery root, peeled and chopped
1 cup parsnips, peeled and chopped
1 cup turnips, peeled and chopped
2 cups Swiss chard leaves, washed and roughly cut
salt and pepper
4 oz veal bacon (or regular bacon)
30+ pieces of ravioli (doesn't have to be potato-leek), store bought or homemade, cooked according to directions

PASTA — SERVES 6

Ravioli con Salsa al Cavolfiore

POTATO AND LEEK RAVIOLI WITH CAULIFLOWER SAUCE

Make a couple extra ravioli in case they break during the cooking!

FOR THE CAULIFLOWER SAUCE

1 Core and coarsely chop the cauliflower. Put it all into a stockpot and cover with the milk.

2 You may not need the entire quart of milk at this point.

3 Bring it to a boil and reduce the heat to a simmer. Add the salt and pepper. Continue to cook on low until the cauliflower is soft and mushy.

4 Remove from heat and purée with immersion blender. Check for consistency. If it is too thin, use cornstarch to thicken.* If it is too thick, use some of the extra milk to thin.

FOR THE VEGETABLE TOPPING

5 Bake strips of bacon in oven until crispy, then crumble and keep at room temperature until ready to use.

6 Warm up about 8–10 oz of cauliflower sauce while preparing vegetables and cooking ravioli.

7 Heat olive oil in pan. Sauté root vegetables for 6-8 minutes. Add Swiss chard and cook until wilted. Season lightly with salt and pepper.

FOR THE PRESENTATION

8 When ravioli are ready, pour some cauliflower sauce on the bottom of the pasta bowl and divide ravioli on it. Then put vegetables on top, and as a final touch, sprinkle some of the crumbled bacon.

**Use a 1:2 ratio of cornstarch to water, for example 1 tsp cornstarch to 2 tsp water. Mix well and gradually add to sauce to thicken.*

WINE PAIRING '01 MARCHESI DI BAROLO BARBERA D'ALBA "RUVEI"

1½	lbs Yukon gold potatoes
1	cup ricotta cheese
½	cup Parmigiano Reggiano cheese, grated
1	egg
½	tsp salt
	pinch of pepper
1	cup olive oil
	all-purpose flour, for dredging

CONTORNO — YIELDS 4-5 SINGLE TORTINO

Tortino di Ricotta e Patate

POTATO CAKE

1 Peel the potatoes and cut them into quarters. Put them in water to boil. When done, drain and purée using ricer or vegetable mill. Put in a bowl and add the remaining ingredients. Mix well.

2 Line a sheet pan with plastic wrap. Turn out the hot mixture onto the pan. Make it flat and even. Cool, covered with plastic wrap.

3 Using a 3-inch cookie cutter, cut circles out of the mix. If you don't have a cookie cutter you can use the top of a glass or just a simple knife to cut squares or triangles. Heat oil in a pan, flour and brown the potato cakes. Set them on a sheet pan and heat in the preheated oven at 450°F for about 15–20 minutes.

- 6 sweet sausages
- 2 whole red peppers, seeded and sliced into ½-inch wide strips
- 3 fennel bulbs, halved, core removed and thinly sliced
- 1 large or 2 small onions, peeled, halved and thinly sliced
- 1 cup olive oil
- 2 lbs pork loin, cut into 2-inch dice
- all-purpose flour, for dredging
- salt and pepper
- 1 cup white wine
- ½ cup tomato sauce or canned crushed tomatoes
- 1 bunch Italian parsley, finely chopped
- vegetable stock
- Grilled Polenta (see page 145)

CARNE — SERVES 6

Stufato di Maiale e Salsiccia

WINTER PORK STEW WITH GRILLED SAUSAGE

Stews are one of my favorite dishes to cook in the winter. I love the good smell my house gets filled with, especially on those cold snowy days! This stew doesn't actually take such a long time to make, it's longer for the preparation than the cooking itself.

If it's winter and you don't feel like grilling the sausage outside, use a griddle or just sear the sausage in a hot pan to get a nice crisp look on the outside, and a more definite flavor!

1 After grilling, cut sausage on a bias about 3 inches long.

2 Heat the oil in a large pot until very hot. Toss pork loin with the flour and strain excess. Sear meat in the pan, getting a nice color all around the meat.

3 Add the cut vegetables and sear them with the meat. Season lightly with the salt and pepper. Add the wine and let it evaporate. Add sausage and stir together.

4 Add the tomato sauce and some vegetable stock to cover half the stew. Let cook slowly, about 20 minutes, letting the juice thicken. Taste and adjust the seasoning if necessary. Add the parsley last to give the stew a nice taste and color.

FOR THE PRESENTATION

5 Place pork stew in soup bowls with sauce. Lay slices of polenta along side.

WINE PAIRING '99 VALDIPIATTA VINO NOBILE DI MONTEPULCIANO "VIGNA ALFIERO"

Polenta

Like bread is to us today, polenta was and still is to the people of Veneto. Originally, it was made in a large copper pot called a "pariolo" and would hang over a burning fire. In my town of Trissino and in all of the Veneto region we are called "polentoni" because polenta is what we are known for. It can be fried, baked, broiled or served with butter and cheese. I love it any way!

As a little girl my favorite day of eating polenta was during the holiday of Santa Lucia. This is a big winter event that falls on December 13th. My nonni on my papá's side would invite the whole family over for lunch. They would slow roast our meal on a big rod, what you would call a rotisserie. Skewered on this would be these little birds called finches, pork meat, lard, sage and pork liver. This would go round and round for like 5 or 6 hours. The birds would get very crunchy and you would eat everything from the beak to the feet! But, the best part was that underneath the big skewer would be a tray that would collect all the drippings and we would put polenta in that big pan. It would absorb all those flavors and get so yummy and crunchy. It was the best thing!

- ¾ cup extra virgin olive oil
- 5 lamb shanks
- 1 tsp salt
- 1 tsp pepper
- 4 cups Burgundy wine
- 1 onion, julienned
- 7 large tomatoes, cut into 8 pieces each
- 4 tbsp fresh rosemary, chopped
- 1½ cups kalamata black olives
- 5 tbsp tomato paste
- 2 tbsp lamb base, if available

CARNE — SERVES 5

Stinco di Agnello Brasato al Vino Rosso

BRAISED LAMB SHANK WITH RED WINE

1 Heat half the oil in a large braising pan. Brown the lamb shanks on all sides. Season with salt and pepper. Add the burgundy and let the alcohol burn off.

2 Meanwhile in another pan, heat the other half of the oil and sauté the onions until almost caramelized. Add the onions to the lamb shanks along with the remaining ingredients. Put the entire braiser in a 350°F degree preheated oven and cover with a sheet pan. If the braiser doesn't fit in your oven, just keep it on the stove, but make sure it simmers.

3 Bake until done, about 2–3 hours. Remove from the oven and allow to cool. Remove shanks out of the sauce.

4 Bring the sauce to a boil and let it simmer to thicken. Make adjustments to seasoning if necessary.

FOR THE PRESENTATION

5 Place lamb shank in bowl. Ladle sauce on top. Serve with roasted potatoes or polenta.

WINE PAIRING '00 VIETTI BAROLO "LAZZARITO"

- 1 lb salt cod, found in Italian market or gourmet stores
- ¾ cup extra virgin olive oil
- 1 onion, minced
- 8 canned anchovy fillets
- 1½ cups whole milk
- ½ bunch Italian parsley, minced
- 1 cup bread flour
- 1 cup Parmigiano Reggiano cheese
- 3 cups heavy cream

PESCE — SERVES 6

Baccalá alla Vicentina

SALT COD VICENTINA STYLE

What great comfort food! This popular dish is made with an assortment of sauces throughout Vicenza. My nonna's version is made with a red sauce and potatoes. Perhaps this is a version of the most famous way Baccalá is cooked in the Veneto. Look for salt cod that is sold loose. The refrigerated kind is not so good – don't buy it! Take care in the rinsing of the fish and enjoy this traditional dish.

This dish is for he who is patient and he who is slightly skilled!

1 Soak and rinse the cod for 2–3 days in a continuous stream of running water to wash off the salt. After the cod is ready, drain and pat the fillets dry. Cut the fillets into 4 x 4-inch pieces.

2 Cook the minced onion in the oil until translucent. Add the anchovies, milk and the parsley. Simmer about 20 minutes. Cool and set aside.

3 Coat a 10 x 13 inch pan with cooking spray. Put the flour into a small bowl and set it next to cod. Arrange the sauce, cheese and cream nearby.

4 Take each piece of cod separately, coat it in flour and set it inside the pan previously brushed with some of the anchovy mixture. Continue with the cod to get one layer down. Cover the layer with some of the mixture. Top that with some of the grated cheese. (You may need a little salt and pepper, very little. Remember, baccalá is still salted!) Start another layer and repeat the above steps. Fill the pan with the cream.

5 Cover the pan with foil and place in a larger pan. Add water halfway up the sides. Bake in 350°F preheated oven for 2–2½ hours. Cool.

FOR THE PRESENTATION

6 Overlap 2 pieces of cod on the plate, drizzle with sauce and serve with grilled polenta.

WINE PAIRING '01 SELVA DEL MORO CHIANTI CLASSICO

For the Marinade

1 cup orange juice concentrate
¼ cup honey
4 8 oz filet mignon
Fennel Custard (see page 143)
Fennel Marmalade (see recipe below)
fennel fronds, for garnish

For the Fennel Marmalade

1 fennel bulb, cleaned, cut, cored and finely diced
3 tbsp red onion, finely diced
¼ cup extra virgin olive oil
1 tbsp lemon juice
1 tbsp sugar
¼ cup frozen orange juice concentrate
1 tsp salt
pinch of black pepper

CARNE — SERVES 4

Filetto all'Arancia

GRILLED ORANGE AND HONEY MARINATED FILET MIGNON

Remember when grilling, honey will caramelize and get a charred color. To get a better result you could grill the filet at a medium-high temperature.

It might be easier for you to make the Fennel Custard and Fennel Marmalade ahead of time. The marmalade can be reheated on the stove. The fennel custard can be reheated in a 450°FF preheated oven for about 20 minutes.

FOR THE MARINADE

1 Mix the ingredients and pour over the filet. Let stand overnight refrigerated.

FOR THE FENNEL MARMALADE

2 Heat oil in large sauté pan. Add the onions and sauté until translucent. Add the fennel. Keep cooking for 3–4 more minutes. Add the rest of the ingredients. Let it cook 5–6 more minutes on low heat.

3 Using the food processor, purée the marmalade a little more. It should still be a little pulpy. Transfer to a storage container until ready to use.

FOR THE PRESENTATION

4 Remove custard from timbale and arrange on side of plate (see page 15). Place filet mignon on the side and cover both with marmalade. Garnish with fennel fronds.

WINE PAIRING '99 SHARDANA VALLI DI PORTO PINO

For the Stuffing

2 heads of garlic, peeled
2 tbsp olive oil
pinch of salt
½ cup olive oil
1 lb Swiss chard leaves, washed and de-stemmed, slice thinly, reserve stems
1 egg
¼ cup breadcrumbs
4 5-6 oz pieces boneless chicken breasts, trimmed of fat

For the Chicken

½ cup olive oil
all-purpose flour, for dredging
vegetable stock
pinch of salt and pepper
1½ cups balsamic vinegar
4 tbsp butter

CARNE — SERVES 4

Pollo Farcito

BALSAMIC BRAISED CHICKEN

Any extra stuffing could be stored in the refrigerator to be used within 3-4 days, or it could be frozen.

FOR THE STUFFING

1 Preheat the oven to 350°F.

2 Combine the garlic, oil and salt in a small pan. Cover with foil and roast in the oven for about 30–45 minutes or until the garlic is soft. Set aside.

3 Heat ½ cup of oil in a large sauté pan. Add the Swiss chard and cook until wilted. Let cool.

4 In a large bowl, combine the whole garlic cloves, the cooled Swiss chard and the remaining ingredients. Mix well.

5 Cut a pocket into the chicken diagonally where you'll insert about ¼ cup of the filling.

FOR THE CHICKEN

6 When you are ready to cook, heat about ½ cup oil in a pan. Dredge the chicken in the flour and add it to the pan. Sear the meat on both sides. It's pretty thick so do not cook it too fast (or on high), otherwise it will burn before it will be thoroughly cooked.

7 After 5 minutes add about 4 tablespoons vegetable stock. While the chicken is cooking, cut the Swiss chard stems into thin strips and add to the pan. Season lightly with salt and pepper and let cook for about 5 more minutes. Add balsamic vinegar. Let simmer slowly. If the chicken is drying out, add a little vegetable stock.

FOR THE PRESENTATION

8 When done place chicken on serving platter that is covered with the Swiss chard.

9 Return the pan to the stove to finish the sauce. Bring it to a boil, adjust seasonings, and add the butter in small pieces, shaking the pan back and forth until you have a nice thick sauce.

10 Pour over the chicken and serve.

WINE PAIRING '01 MARCARINI NEBBIOLO "LASARIN"

½ cup extra virgin olive oil
1½ lbs veal scaloppini meat, sliced into thin strips, ¼ inch wide
1 cup parsnips, peeled and diced
1 cup turnips, peeled and diced
1 cup celery root
all-purpose flour, for dredging
4 oz mascarpone cheese
2 tbsp Italian parsley, chopped
1 tsp salt
1 tsp black pepper
1-2 sheets of frozen puff pastry
1 egg
Cauliflower Sauce (see page 154)
1 bunch Swiss chard, leaves and stems julienne

CARNE — SERVES 6

Vitello in Pasta Sfoglia

VEAL IN PUFF PASTRY IN A CAULIFLOWER SAUCE

Veal is probably the second most prominent meat, following pork, in the Veneto region. This recipe takes several steps to get it ready for assembly. C'mon, don't be scared to do the work! You will be happy you did. The good thing is that you can prepare it 1-2 days before you are planning on serving it.

Pasta sfoglia is puff pastry!

1 Heat half the oil in a pan. Flour the meat and brown it in the oil. Season with salt and pepper. Set aside.

2 Heat the rest of the oil in another pan and sauté the vegetables until they are done. Put the meat and vegetables in a large pan, fold in the mascarpone, parsley, salt and pepper. Allow to cool before proceeding.

3 Sprinkle work surface with flour. Roll puff pastry to ⅛-inch thick. Cut it so that you have 6 pieces, approximately 6 x 7 inches.

4 Put 6 oz filling in the center of each sheet. Gather the corners together, stretching over the filling. Turn the packages over and brush each with cracked egg that has been slightly beaten. Feel free to decorate the top with the leftover scraps of puff pastry.

5 Preheat oven to 450°F. Bake for about 25-30 minutes or until pastry turns golden brown.

FOR THE PRESENTATION

6 Ladle ¼-½ cup of Cauliflower Sauce on the plate. Place pastry bundle on top and garnish with sautéed Swiss chard leaves and blanched Swiss chard stems, cut in sticks.

WINE PAIRING '03 ARGIOLAS "PERDERA"

IMPASTO — YIELDS FIVE, 6 OZ PIZZAS

Pasta per la Pizza

PIZZA DOUGH

Just like bruschetterie, we have pizzerie when you are in the mood for pizza. There are tons of varieties of toppings; for sure you can eat it with whatever you want, but I still like the simple mozzarella, tomatoes, fresh basil and a little Parmesan cheese. Semplice e buona!

If you don't have a dough mixer, it's okay to combine the dough by hand in a large salad bowl and knead on a work surface. It will take you some time; you must be patient!

- 2 cups warm water + 2 tbsp
- 2 tsp salt
- 4 tsp sugar
- 2 tsp dry active yeast
- 6 tbsp vegetable oil
- 1¾ cups semolina flour
- 3½ cups bread flour

1 Run the tap for hot water and adjust to lukewarm. Measure out 2 cups and pour into bowl. Add the sugar, salt, yeast and oil. Stir well.

2 Measure out the two flours and add to the bowl of a mixer. Connect the bowl to machine and using a dough hook, mix for 15 minutes.

3 Flour a spot on the table and turn the dough out of the bowl. Work dough to a smooth ball. Portion into 7 oz pieces. Roll them into balls and line them up on sprayed sheet trays. Cover the trays. Allow balls to rise 20 minutes before rolling.

4 Roll out pizza about 10 inches round. Use some flour for dusting while rolling and some flour on the paper to avoid having the pizza stick. You could roll out pizzas and store in sheet tray with paper in between for up to 5 days before using.

4	egg yolks
½	cup sugar
½	quart heavy cream
2	shots regular espresso
1	tbsp chocolate powder

DOLCE — SERVES 6

Cappuccino Crème Brûlée

CAPPUCCINO FLAVORED EGG CUSTARD

Be careful, these don't get as firm in the oven as regular crème brûlée so they may look a little soft when they're actually done.

1 Whisk together the yolks and sugar, then add heavy cream.

2 In a separate container whisk together the espresso and chocolate powder. Add this to the cream.

3 Divide into six, 5 oz oval dishes. Place dishes in larger pan and fill halfway up the sides with water (water bath). Bake in preheated 350°F oven about 20–25 minutes, until set. Allow to cool, then place in refrigerator to completely chill.

4 To serve, sprinkle evenly with raw sugar and caramelize with a torch.

WINE PAIRING '05 VIETTI MOSCATO D'ASTI "CASCINETTA"

For the Procedure

2 tbsp all-purpose flour
1 tsp kosher salt
1 tbsp baking powder
1 tbsp chocolate powder
½ cup sugar
¼ cup brown sugar
2 cans whole chestnuts, drained and puréed
3 eggs
¼ cup honey
½ cup extra virgin olive oil
¾ cup dried cherries
½ cup golden raisins
1 cup walnut pieces, toasted and chopped
½ cup pine nuts, toasted and chopped

Syrup

1 cup honey
1 orange
½ cup Vin Santo

DOLCE – YIELDS 1 CAKE

Castagnaccio

CHESTNUT CAKE

My sorella Graziella and I loved to go out in the woods with my papá. My fratello, Paolo, was too little and my mamma was busy in the kitchen. Sometimes we went just for fun, exploring, but mostly to look for mushrooms, figs, and chestnuts. Of course, the search was most fun when we were successful. Chestnuts have spiky, hard shells that we removed in the woods to see if the inside was good. Then we had to deliver them to my mamma to boil or put in the fire to roast. This cake certainly brings home those memories.

If you can't find Vin Santo, use Moscato instead.

FOR THE PROCEDURE

1 Combine the dry ingredients together.

2 In another bowl, combine the chestnuts with the eggs, honey and olive oil. Gradually stir the dry into the wet, finally adding the cherries, raisins and nuts. Pour into a greased 9-inch spring-form pan and bake at 350°F for 20 minutes. The cake should puff slightly when done.

SYRUP

3 Peel a few strips of zest from the orange and combine in a small pan with the honey and Vin Santo. Bring to a boil. Then, remove from the heat and brush cake with the syrup as soon as it comes out of the oven.

WINE PAIRING '04 VILLA GIADA BRACCHETTO "AMIS"

3	oranges, with skin
6	eggs
1¼	cups sugar
½	cup chocolate powder
1	tbsp baking powder, heaping
½	tsp baking soda
2	cups blanched slivered almonds, ground

DOLCE — YIELDS 1 9-INCH CAKE

Torta D'arancio e Cioccolato

CHOCOLATE ORANGE CAKE

1 Boil the oranges until they're soft to the touch. Purée them whole in a food processor, and allow to cool.

2 Line the bottom of a spring-form pan with paper and coat with cooking spray.

3 Meanwhile, in large bowl mix together the eggs, sugar and chocolate powder. Whisk in the baking powder and baking soda.

4 Stir in the ground almonds and orange purée. Mix well and pour into pan.

5 Bake at 350°F for 45 minutes.

6 Serve with orange flavor vanilla sauce. Follow recipe for Vanilla Cream Sauce (see page 129), adding zest of 1 orange to the cream.

WINE PAIRING '03 SAN RUSTICO RECIOTO DELLA AMARONE CLASSICO "VIGNETO GASO"

Bottom layer

1 recipe Brownies with Walnuts (see page 172)

For the Inner Layer

½ cup chocolate chips
2 tbsp unsalted butter

For the Crust

1¼ cups ground walnuts
1¼ cups graham cracker crumbs
1½ tbsp chocolate powder
1½ tbsp brown sugar
3 tbsp unsalted butter
4 tbsp chocolate chips

For the Top Layer of Mousse

1½ cups chocolate chips
2 tbsp unsalted butter
½ cup heavy cream
3 egg yolks
1 cup heavy cream

DOLCE — YIELDS 1 CAKE, 12-15 PORTIONS

Torta con Mousse al Cioccolato

CHOCOLATE MOUSSE CAKE

Big favorite at Paesano's!

Lo so, lo so, una gran rottura di palle!

It will take you all day to do it! So what, choose a rainy, cold day or get your husband out of the house with the kids and you stay at home baking.

FOR THE INNER LAYER

1 Melt chocolate chips and butter together in a double boiler on the stove. Spread this thinly over the brownies. It will act as the "glue" for the next layer, the crust.

FOR THE CRUST

2 Combine the walnuts, graham cracker crumbs, chocolate powder and brown sugar in a large bowl.

3 Melt chocolate chips and butter together in a double boiler on the stove. Add this to the other ingredients combining it with your hands to distribute the chocolate and butter evenly.

4 Take this crust mixture and press it down evenly over the whole pan of brownies that was spread with chocolate layer.

5 Cover the pan with plastic and place in the freezer while you prepare the last layer.

FOR THE TOP LAYER OF MOUSSE

6 In a large bowl over a double boiler, melt together the chocolate, butter and ½ cup of cream.

7 Meanwhile, whip the other cup of cream in the mixer and set aside.

8 When the chocolate mixture is melted, whisk it well to eliminate any lumps. Whisk in the egg yolks. If you have time, let this mixture sit in the freezer for a little while to cool, whisking it periodically. Otherwise, continue with the recipe.

9 Gradually fold the chocolate mixture into the whipped cream, folding it until there are no lumps of cream left. This isn't absolutely necessary, but it helps set the crumbly layer.

10 Finally, remove pan from freezer and top with mousse. Can refreeze again at this point.

11 Cut and place on serving dish while still frozen, then allow to reach room temperature before serving.

½ cup chocolate chips
1½ sticks unsalted butter, softened
3 eggs, beaten
1 cup sugar
¾ cup all-purpose flour
1 cup walnuts, chopped

DOLCE — YIELDS 1 PAN OF BROWNIES

"Brownies" con le Noci

BROWNIES WITH WALNUTS

1 Coat 12 x 9 inch pan with cooking spray, line with parchment paper and set aside.

2 In a double boiler, melt the chocolate and butter together. Transfer to a large bowl.

3 Add the eggs to the chocolate and whisk well. Then add the sugar, flour and walnuts.

4 Pour the batter into prepared pan and bake at 350°F for 20–25 minutes.

WINE PAIRING '04 MICHELE CHIARLO MOSCATO D'ASTI "NIVOLE"

4 cups breadcrumbs
6 cups milk
2 tbsp liquor (Grand Marnier)
7 eggs
¾ cup flour
1¼ cups raisins
½ cup candied fruit, cut into small pieces
1½ cups sugar
1 lemon (zest only)
pinch of salt
powdered sugar

DOLCE — SERVES 12-15

Puttana

BREAD AND RAISIN TORTE

My nonna Giovanna's party cake! Simple and rustic!

1 Mix breadcrumbs, milk and liquor all together a day before you are planning to bake the cake.

2 Next morning, lightly beat the eggs, add them to the bread mixture. Then add, flour, raisins, candied fruit, sugar, lemon zest and salt.

3 Butter a 9 x 12 inch baking pan, and coat it with bread-crumbs. Pour in the batter.

4 Bake in a preheated oven at 375°F for about 1½ hours. Insert a toothpick in it to see if the batter is dry, if not, cook a little longer.

5 While baking, the cake might puff up, but it will go down when it is out of the oven. Turn it upside down and cut it in small pieces. Serve while it is still warm. Sprinkle heavily with powdered sugar.

WINE PAIRING '98 MACULAN "TORCOLATO"

- 2 pink grapefruit
- 3 oranges
- 3 blood oranges
- 2 limes
- 1 cup sliced almonds
- 1 tsp ground cinnamon
- ½ cup raw turbinado bulk sugar or brown sugar

DOLCE — SERVES 6

Gratin di Agrumi

CITRUS GRATIN

1 Peel and section the grapefruit and oranges. Add to them the zest of the limes and the cinnamon and mix.

2 Divide the fruit into oval dishes used for crème brûlée, top with ground almonds and sugar. Put under the broiler to make a crust. Serve immediately.

WINE PAIRING '04 TINTERO MOSCATO D'ASTI "SORI GRAMELLA"

Condimenti

DRESSINGS

Salads in Italy are usually very basic – just mixed greens! Salad dressing to us is always olive oil, vinegar, salt and pepper. So, you can imagine when I came to America the concept of salad dressing was very new to me. However, I have created some very tasty dressings over the years that I really like and that our customers enjoy. I know you will too.

Cucumber Dressing *(summer)*

1 seedless English cucumber, peeled and cut into small pieces
¼ cup olive oil
¼ cup extra virgin olive oil
1 lime, zest and juice
¼ tsp black pepper

Purée all ingredients together.

Lemon Citronette *(summer/spring)*

2 small lemons, zested and juiced
1 tbsp Dijon mustard
1 cup extra virgin olive oil
pinch of salt and pepper

Mix lemons and mustard together, whisk in the oil slowly.
Season with salt and pepper.

Maple-Orange Vinaigrette *(winter)*

½ cup red wine vinegar
½ cup good quality maple syrup
¼ cup frozen concentrated orange juice
juice from 1 lemon
½ cup olive oil
pinch of salt and pepper

Combine first four ingredients, whisk in the oil slowly.
Season with salt and pepper.

Chestnut Honey Dressing *(winter)*

2½ oz chestnuts, may use canned if necessary
⅛ cup honey
⅛ cup balsamic vinegar
1¼ cups olive oil
⅛ cup chilled water
pinch of salt and pepper

If using fresh chestnuts, you must boil them until soft, then peel and purée them. Add all the ingredients except the oil in a mixing bowl. Using a whisk, slowly incorporate the oil.

Balsamic Glaze *(any season)*

1 cup balsamic vinegar
¼ cup brown sugar

Combine vinegar and sugar in a saucepan and bring to a boil.
Continue boiling until contents reduces by 1½.
It will last a long time in the refrigerator.

Lemon-Thyme Dressing *(summer/spring)*

1 tbsp fresh thyme, chopped
1 lemon, zested and juiced
pinch of salt and pepper
1 cup mayonnaise
¾ cup buttermilk

Mix all the ingredients together and store in a container in the refrigerator until ready to use.

Lemon Mustard Citronette *(summer/spring)*

1½ lemons, zested and juiced
4 tbsp Dijon mustard
¼ tsp ground black pepper
1 cup olive oil
2 tbsp shallots, finely chopped

Mix all but oil together, then slowly whisk in the oil.
Put in covered container and refrigerate until ready to use.

Cinzano Vinaigrette *(summer)*

½ bottle sweet vermouth
2 tbsp fresh thyme, destemmed and minced
¾ cup raspberry vinegar
1 tsp kosher salt
½ tsp ground black pepper
1 cup extra virgin olive oil

Heat the vermouth in a sauce pan to reduce it by half. Let cool.

In a mixing bowl, combine the cooled vermouth with the minced rosemary, the vinegar and the salt and pepper. Slowly, using a whisk, add the oil. Pour in a container and refrigerate until ready to use.

Honey and Apple Cider Vinaigrette *(fall)*

½ cup cider vinegar
½ cup honey
½ tsp Dijon mustard
pinch of salt
½ cup olive oil
½ cup extra virgin olive oil

Combine the apple cider vinegar with the honey in a mixing bowl. Add the mustard, salt and mix well.

Slowly drizzle in the oil and using a hand whisk incorporate it to the mix to avoid later separating.

Black Grape Dressing *(fall)*

1 lbs black seedless grapes, destemmed and washed
¼ cup cold water
¼ cup balsamic vinegar
½ tsp salt
pinch of ground black pepper
pinch of ground nutmeg
½ cup olive oil

Put the grapes in a saucepan and heat them up until they release their juices. Simmer for 5–7 minutes.

Purée the grapes with the hand mixer or food processor. Cool. Measure out about 1⅔ cups of grape purée and add the water. Add the remaining ingredients.

Again, using a hand mixer blend all together. If you have to use the food processor add the oil at the end very slowly with the machine running.

Refrigerate until ready to use.

Index

CANEDERLI
DA
BRODO
€ 8.50
CAPELACCI
CON
RADICCHIO

BROLO DI
CAMPOFIORIN
MASI